Bury the Dead

Bury the Dead

Stories of Death and Dying, Resistance and Discipleship

Edited by
Laurel Dykstra

 CASCADE *Books* · Eugene, Oregon

BURY THE DEAD
Stories of Death and Dying, Resistance and Discipleship

Copyright © 2013 Wipf and Stock Publishers. All rights reserved. Except for brief quotations in critical publications or reviews, no part of this book may be reproduced in any manner without prior written permission from the publisher. Write: Permissions, Wipf and Stock Publishers, 199 W. 8th Ave., Suite 3, Eugene, OR 97401.

Cascade Books
An Imprint of Wipf and Stock Publishers
199 W. 8th Ave., Suite 3
Eugene, OR 97401

www.wipfandstock.com

ISBN 13: 978-1-62032-213-0

Cataloguing-in-Publication data:

Bury the dead : stories of death and dying, resistance and discipleship / edited by Laurel Dykstra.

xx + 160 pp. ; 23 cm. ; Includes bibliographical references.

ISBN 13: 978-1-62032-213-0

1. Death—Religious aspects—Christianity. 2. Death and burial—Religious aspects. 3. Death and life. I. Title.

BT825 B85 2013

Manufactured in the U.S.A.

Unless otherwise indicated biblical citations are from the New Revised Standard Version of the Bible, copyright © 1989, Division of Christian Education of the National Council of the Churches of Christ in the United States of America. Used by permission. All rights reserved.

All royalties from the sale of this book go to support Word and World Discipleship Schools and Mentorship Program.

To all who have taught and studied, mentored and been mentored, rooted their struggle in movement history, prayed, acted, cried, danced, risked and told the truth at Word and World discipleship schools, programs, street actions, and retreats; and to all who will do so in the future: *In the face of death, live humanly. In the middle of chaos, celebrate the Word.* Amen.

The dead are never gone,
they are in the breast of a woman,
they are in the crying child,
in the flaming firebrand.
The dead are not in earth:
they are in the dying fire,
the weeping grasses,
whimpering rocks,
they are in the forest,
they are in the house,
the dead are not dead.

—BIRAGO DIOP

Contents

Part II: Remembrance and Resistance

Acknowledgments

TELLING STORIES IS A community undertaking; this collection of stories began in community and a web of relationship brought it to the form you hold in your hands. Thanks to the Word and World mentorship group where these conversations began, thanks to the W&W board and especially to board chair Mike Boucher for his faithfulness and dedication.

To write about death is to enter into a sacred and dangerous territory. To all the contributors I stand in awe of your courage in writing and your generosity in the editing process. I honor too, those carrying stories who were not able to share them here, among them Ruby Sales, Sue Ablao, and James Loney. Although your voices are not heard here you are far from silent.

Thanks to friends and supporters who freely shared knowledge, skills, and information: Julia MacRae for translation, Bruce Triggs for editing advice, Bill Wylie-Kellermann for all my Stringfellow needs, Ched Myers for cheerleading and e-mail addresses, and Bartimaeus Cooperative Ministries for promoting the project.

To those who perform the often unsung tasks of prompter, electronic correspondent, pre-editor, message taker, and calendar keeper to a partner, friend or community member: Laura Karlin, Joyce Hobson Johnson, Mike Wisniewski and Joyce Hollyday—I sing you.

Deep and humble acknowledgment of the many communities—especially indigenous, racialized, queer and gender queer, disabled, and impoverished communities—that live every day in resistance to the Power of death. You inspire this work.

Thank you to the team at Cascade Books for calm competence and professionalism.

And thank you to my crazy family, bio and chosen, for everything.

Several contributions to this volume were published previously in books, periodicals, and websites. The kind permissions of the following authors, publishers, and copyright holders are gratefully acknowledged:

Versions of "Thoughts on Burying My Mother, Brother, and of course, John," by Jeff Dietrich have appeared as "Blessed Are Those Who Mourn," *Catholic Agitator* 24/2 (1993) 3, 6; and as "Thoughts on Burying My Mother, Brother and, of course, John," *National Catholic Reporter*, October 22, 1993, 20.

"To Die at the Catholic Worker," by Kieran Prather first appeared in the *Catholic Agitator* 23/2 (1993) 1–2.

A version of "May the Angels Guide You into Heaven," by Jeff Dietrich, first appeared in the *Catholic Agitator* 25/1 (1995). The version included in this volume includes excerpts from Dietrich's "Kieran's Mission Fulfilled," which also appeared in volume 25 of the *Catholic Agitator*.

"Who Will Roll Away the Stone?," by Ched Myers, was first published as "He Goes Before You to Galilee," *Catholic Agitator* 25/1 (1995) and is based on Ched Myers, *Who Will Roll Away the Stone? Discipleship Queries for First-World Christians* (Maryknoll: Orbis, 1994), 410–12.

A version of "Secondlines," by Jordan Flaherty first appeared in Jordan Flaherty, *Floodlines: Community and Resistance from Katrina to the Jena Six* (Chicago: Haymarket, 2010), 7–9.

"Deadly Betrayal . . . and a Return to Childhood Faith" first appeared in the *Witness* 84/3 (2001) 27–29 and is reprinted by permission of The Archives of the Episcopal Church.

An excerpt from "*Oda al hombre sencillo,*" by Pablo Neruda is reprinted with permission from the Neruda Foundation.

"A Peaceful Warrior Lives On in Us," by Frida Berrigan, first appeared December 9, 2011, on the *Waging Nonviolence* website under a Creative Commons Attribution-Share Alike 3.0 United States License.

Contributors

Frida Berrigan is a columnist for *Waging Nonviolence*. She serves on the board of the War Resisters League and helped found Witness Against Torture. She and her family live in New London, Connecticut.

Mary Bradford is a hospice social worker in Tacoma, Washington. She lived for ten years in Brownsville, Texas, where she taught in a Catholic school, helped establish La Posada soup kitchen, and assisted Central American refugees. Upon returning to the Northwest, she became the director of Nativity House, a drop-in center in Tacoma, Washington, and later worked as a prison chaplain and a pastoral social justice worker at St. Leo Parish, where she is currently a member. Mary writes a bilingual blog (www.gringavieja.blogspot.com); she is deeply grateful to be part of a community of friends and spiritual soulmates—many of whom are affiliated with St. Leo's or the Tacoma Catholic Worker—who work for justice while striving to maintain a sense of humor. Mary considers her hospice work to be reverse midwifery and she feels blessed to be able to enter into people's lives at such a holy, vulnerable time.

Murphy Davis is a Presbyterian pastor. She has been, since 1977, the Director of Southern Prison Ministry in Georgia. She and her husband, Eduard Loring founded The Open Door Community, a "Protestant Catholic Worker Community" in downtown Atlanta, and have lived there with and among formerly homeless and formerly imprisoned sisters and brothers since 1981. Her contribution to this anthology includes materials from her forthcoming book, *Surely Goodness and Mercy: A Journey into Illness and Solidarity*.

Jeff Dietrich is an activist and writer who lives and serves on Los Angeles' Skid Row as a member of the Los Angeles Catholic Worker community.

He has dedicated his life and writing to the plight of the poor and homeless, and to challenging the political and social systems that help maintain
and perpetuate poverty and injustice. He is the editor of the bi-monthly
newspaper, the *Catholic Agitator*, to which he also is a frequent contributor. Other journals and newspapers that have published his writing
include the *Los Angeles Times* and the *Catholic National Reporter*. A collection of his essays was published in book form in 2011 titled *Broken
and Shared: Food, Dignity, and the Poor on Los Angeles' Skid Row*. He also
is a contributor to another book, *In Possession of Shakespeare: Writing
into Nothing*, which will be published in spring of 2012.

Laurel Dykstra is a community-based scholar with a long history in
intentional communities and the radical discipleship movement. Her
justice work focuses on issues of urban poverty; the activism of children,
youth and families; challenging white privilege; and Queer and gender-
Queer participation and resistance in churches. She is the author of *Set
Them Free: The Other Side of Exodus* (Orbis, 2002), *Uncle Aiden* (Baby
Bloc, 2005), and co-editor, with Ched Myers of *Liberating Biblical Study*
(Cascade Books, 2011). She is a collective member if the Interfaith Institute for Justice, Peace and Social Movements and a member of the
Christian activist group Streams of Justice. Laurel lives with her not so
traditional family in a housing co-op in the Downtown Eastside of Van-
couver, BC where she is exploring the vocation of neighbour. She was
recently ordained priest in the Anglican Church of Canada's Diocese of
New Westminster.

Elaine Enns lives in Oak View, California, and co-directs Bartimaeus
Cooperative Ministries with her partner Ched Myers. Elaine has worked
for over twenty years in the field of restorative justice and conflict transformation as victim-offender facilitator, consultant, educator, and trainer
(www.bcm-net.org). Elaine and Ched co-authored a two volume project
*Ambassadors of Reconciliation: New Testament Reflections and Diverse
Christian Practices of Restorative Justice and Peacemaking* (Orbis, 2009).
In 2002, Elaine and Ched, together with the Guadalupe Catholic Worker,
provided four months of hospice for their mentor, Ladon Sheats.

Andrea Ferich is currently the Executive Director of the Penns Valley
Conservation Association in Centre County, Pennsylvania, in the ridge
and valley region. She lives for peace through sustainable community development, food system security, the arts, and loving fiercely. She enjoys

gardening with children and growing imaginations. Andrea left Camden, New Jersey in November 2012 and is reimmersing herself in connection with the pristine stillness of the wild. She has been visiting various farms and has found a deep peace naming ephemeral unnamed springs of the karst topography. Currently she is planning woodcock habitat restoration projects and helping to stitch together a thriving local economy, so please visit. Visit her blog at aferich.blogspot.com for a free environmental justice garden toolkit and to connect with a liturgy of the soil and the saints.

Jordan Flaherty is a journalist based in New Orleans and a producer on Fault Lines, the flagship current affairs news program on Al Jazeera. He was the first writer to bring the story of the Jena Six to a national audience, and his award-winning reporting from the Gulf Coast has been featured in a range of outlets including the *New York Times*, *Washington Post*, *Mother Jones*, and Argentina's *Clarin* newspaper. He has appeared as a guest on a wide range of television and radio shows, including CNN Morning, Anderson Cooper 360, CNN Headline News, Democracy Now, RT, News and Notes, and various programs on National Public Radio and Air America. He is author of the book *Floodlines: Community and Resistance from Katrina to the Jena Six* (Haymarket, 2010).

Joyce Hollyday, who lives in community on a farm in the mountains of Western North Carolina, is a co-founder and co-pastor of Circle of Mercy, an ecumenical congregation in Asheville (www.circleofmercy.org). She is the author of several books, including *Clothed with the Sun: Biblical Women, Social Justice, and Us* and *Then Shall Your Light Rise: Spiritual Formation and Social Witness*. A co-founder of Witness for Peace in Nicaragua and the itinerant school for faith-based activists known as Word and World, Joyce has also served as an Associate Conference Minister for the United Church of Christ, Associate Editor of *Sojourners* magazine, chaplain to children with cancer, and pastor on Georgia's death row. She is at work on a novel based on her mother's journey with Alzheimer's and a book about Truth and Reconciliation processes in South Africa, North Carolina, and Canada. Her blog about community can be found at www.seekingcommunity.ca.

Rev. Dr. Nelson N. Johnson has been active in the movement for social and economic justice since high school in the late 1950s. A survivor of a Klan shooting in 1979, he was a powerful contributor to the Greensboro Truth and Reconciliation Commission. Rev. Johnson centers his efforts on facilitating a process of comprehensive community building, which include a convergence of racial and ethnic diversity, social and economic justice, and genuine participatory democracy. At the Beloved Community Center where he is co-founder and director, he and his colleagues attempt to bring together the homeless, the imprisoned, impoverished neighborhoods, and other disenfranchised groups in the spirit of mutual support and community. Guided by his three-part emphasis of diversity, justice and democracy, Rev. Johnson is actively building relationships with and providing leadership within organized labor, faith groups and other public and private community organizations.

Tom Karlin is a peace activist, Navy veteran, former Trappist monk, and grandfather of eight. He was the tenth child of fifteen in a Volga German Catholic farming family in central Kansas. Tom met his wife Ida while a Jesuit Volunteer Corps carpenter in Alaska. Together they raised four children near Mt. Rainier until Ida died of cancer in 1994. Tom has focused on creating intentional Christian community, homesteading with sustainable practices, and working for social justice. As a conscientious objector, Tom shaped his woodworking business to never owe taxes that would fund US military policy. Tom was arrested five times for civil resistance to nuclear weapons, and served four months in federal prison. After seven years in the Tacoma Catholic Worker, Tom and wife Laura left to vigil with three of his siblings dying of cancer. The couple now lives with Laura's aging mother in Lakewood, Washington. Tom is a contributor to Rosalie Riegel's anthology on civil disobedience, *Doing Time for Peace: Resistance, Family, and Community* (Vanderbilt, 2013).

Ched Myers lives in Oak View, California, and co-directs Bartimaeus Cooperative Ministries with his partner Elaine Enns. Ched, whose many publications are available at www.ChedMyers.org, focuses on building biblical literacy, church renewal, and faith-based witness for social justice. His most recent publication, *Our God is Undocumented: Biblical Faith and Immigrant Justice,* is co-authored with Matthew Colwell (Orbis, 2012). Ched and Elaine co-authored a two volume project *Ambassadors of Reconciliation: New Testament Reflections and Diverse Christian Practices of Restorative Justice and Peacemaking* (Orbis, 2009). In 2002, Ched and Elaine, together with the Guadalupe Catholic Worker, provided four months of hospice for their mentor, Ladon Sheats.

Elizabeth Nicolas (Liz) is a Haitian-American and native New Yorker who has lived in Philadelphia for the past twelve years. She has supported and worked with several Philly non-profits focused on issues such as homeless advocacy, education, community development and urban renewal. In November 2012, Liz resigned from her position as a litigation attorney representing large corporate clients to fully pursue her passion and commitment to advocate for individuals on the margins. She reads a lot and recently, has been very interested in biblical scholarship on intersections of race, gender, politics and sexuality.

Kieran Prather (1947–1994) joined the Los Angeles Catholic Worker community in September, 1991. A writer and teacher, a beloved member of local recovery and gay communities, a good listener with a brilliant intellect, he brought many gifts to our community. He was invaluable during difficult community meetings, helping us, with a quiet dignity, listen to each person's point of view. He died of AIDS on Christmas Day, 1994. We miss him still.

Pablo Ruiz is a Chilean human rights activist and journalist who lives in Santiago, Chile. He is a former political prisoner who was arrested and tortured in 1989 and spent two years in prison. During the 1990s he worked with the Committee Against Impunity, seeking to bring to trial military who had committed human rights abuses during the Pinochet dictatorship. In 1999 he joined the Kamarikun Human Rights Committee and in 2002 joined the Human Rights Education Team of Amnesty International Chile. In 2000 Pablo spearheaded Kamarikun's efforts to seek the withdrawal of Chile from the School of the Americas (SOA). He organized SOA Watch delegations to Chile and joined SOA Watch delegations to Colombia, Panamá and Ecuador. Currently, Pablo participates in the Ethics Commission against Torture, the Oscar Romero Committee and works as the Communications Coordinator for SOA Watch's Partnership America Latina.

Eda Ruhiye Uca is founding director of Hosanna! People's Seminary (H!PS). At H!PS she develops and facilitates opportunities to connect geographically dispersed stakeholders in Christian and interfaith anti-oppression training and community building. A first generation American of Middle Eastern heritage, Eda's first spoken language is Turkish and her first spiritual language is Islam. She is a member of the Evangelical Lutheran Church in America and has lived in radical Christian (and non-religious) intentional communities. Eda is a regular contributor to *Jesus Radicals* and *New Women, New Church*, in addition to being a student at The Episcopal Divinity School. Eda's interests include missiology, theodicy, third wave feminism, Middle Eastern liberation theology, postcolonial theory, science and theology, and the intersectionality of oppressions. She lives in Cambridge, Massachusetts.

Bill Wylie-Kellermann is a writer and nonviolent community activist, a Methodist pastor serving St Peter's Episcopal Church Detroit. For more than two decades he lived fully partnered with Jeanie Wylie, engaged journalist, editor, and film-maker. She crossed over to God in 2005, having lived eight years with an aggressive brain tumor. Their daughters, Lydia and Lucy, are, with her, witnesses to resurrection. Bill has authored *Seasons of Faith and Conscience: Reflections on Liturgical Direct Action* (reprinted, Wipf & Stock, 2008) and edited *A Keeper of the Word* (Eerdmans, 1994). His forthcoming books include *William Stringfellow* and *Dying Humanly: The Resurrected Life of Jeanie Wylie-Kellermann*. As co-founder of Word and World: A Peoples' School, adjunct faculty at SCUPE –Chicago and at Marygrove's MA/Social Justice in Detroit, his teaching and writing are generally framed by a theology of the "principalites." In Jesus, he bets his life on the gospel nonviolence, good news to the poor, Word made flesh, and freedom from the power of death.

Lydia Wylie-Kellermann was born and raised in the Catholic Worker movement in Detroit. She lost her mother on December 31, 2005 at age nineteen. Lydia and her partner Erinn live in the Jeanie Wylie Community (named for her mother), a community in the Catholic Worker tradition focusing on urban agriculture and support for undocumented families in Detroit, Michigan.

Introduction

THIS BOOK BEGAN WITH a phone conversation during the Word and World Mentorship program in 2011. Lydia Wylie-Kellermann was struggling to write about her mother. The luminous Jeanie Wylie-Kellerman, writer, activist, and discipleship movement stalwart, was diagnosed with brain cancer when Lydia was twelve and died when she was nineteen. Meanwhile I, her supposed mentor, was trying and failing with words and paper to placte the spirits of neighbors—women dead from the complications of prolonged and untreated racism and poverty—who I can only describe as haunting me. Lydia and I were carrying stories of death and grief in a culture that is emphatic in its refusal to hear them. Reflecting later on the conversation, I realized that the two of us were actually connected to a network of individuals and communites on the radical Christian left who had, for many years, in hospice rooms, war zones, and prison cells, been attending to the work of death and dying. Perhaps we could draw on this wealth of support and resources and carve out a place to tell our stories and invite others to do the same.

When I sent round an exploratory e-mail to Lydia and some other likely suspects, asking, "What if we made a collection of stories about dying, community, and resistance, would you write something?" the response was immediate; by next morning six people had promised to write, three had attached sample chapters. So the project began, characterized by a kind of kairos urgency, a sense that the time was right. Murphy Davis of the Open Door Community put it this way, "One of these fine days I'll die like they've been predicting all along and my opportunity to write about it will be over, so I'm sort of racing the clock!" Others described relief, recognition, and excitement at finding a place they didn't know they had been looking for—a place where words like AIDS, dementia, suicide, racism, prison, and grief needn't be whispered or avoided.

The result of our conversations and collaboration is the amazing patchwork of stories you now hold: stories from the street, the bedside, the front line, and the academy. Some are fresh, even raw, others polished and professional, a few have been told before but bear repeating, and—because dying happens in community—a few are different versions of the same story. The words of bloggers, journalists, new writers, students, lawyers, biblical scholars, movement veterans, and pastors form a sometimes lovely, sometimes awkward juxtapostion of voices and perspectives where inclusion trumps stylistic unity.

Contributors this anthology come mostly from a loosely connected network of movements and communities on the Christian left in North America: Catholic Worker, L'Arche, Radical Discipleship, Occupy, Anti-War, School of the Americas Watch, Civil Rights, Christian Peacemaker Teams, and others. In a sense this is movement history documented by activists aged mid-twenties to nearly eighty. While some voices and stories are amplified, others are missing, among the absent are: communites of color doing hospice work, the disability rights movement, prisoners and those on death row, veterans and families of deceased soldiers, families of murder victims. Some of these absences represent places where grief is too fresh for the telling, or communities so fully engaged in living and resistance that documenting the work is not a priority. Other absences are not as easily excused; they are simply the weakness of this collection and the biases of the communities that created it. This volume is not intended to be a definitive statement but is an admittedly awkward overture, a conversation starter, and hopefully a catalyst for continued conversations.

In his classic volume *The Prophetic Imagination*, Walter Brueggemann describes the prophet as unafraid to look at death, to engage with and confront it. This book documents eighteen modern prophets' engagement with death—in cancer wards, at military training academies, on death row, and in racialized neighborhoods. The title, *Bury the Dead*, evokes the corporal Work of Mercy, and its biblical prescidents; the long-held understanding that all Christians have a real and practical obligation to the dead. Whether building coffins or building labor and anti-racism alliances, the book's contributors live out this obligation.

Bury the Dead is divided into two sections. Death and Burial includes accounts of hospice—midwifing the dying—and green burial practices; Remembrance and Resistance is about campaignings, movements, and social structures. The chapters are arranged according to connections between their themes, authors, and subjects, but most could fit in either half of the book. Although it is tempting to characterize the first half of the book as more personal and the second half as more political, the stories themselves won't allow it.

In the first offerings to the volume, Lydia and Bill Wylie-Kellermann's achingly physical accounts of their engagement with the dying of a beloved mother and partner, are inseperable from the peace and justice movement in which all three lived. When Ladon Sheats was dying virtually penniless, his community of care rose up from the picket lines, prison cells, and community kitchens of actions past. Frida Berrigan's speech on the living and dying of Phil Berrigan, her father and father of the North American peace movement, would easily fit in the first half of the book, but for the fact that it was delivered in Zuccotti Park in the heart of the Occupy movement. And as I write I hear the echoes of Murphy Davis' partner Ed Loring, bellowing in hospital corridors, street corners, and prayer meetings, "Cancer is Political!"

Rather than personal and political, I suggest two ways of understanding how the book is arranged. The first is that in the broadest strokes, the stories move from accounts of the deaths of individuals—family members and loved ones—to the stories of death of large numbers and the pervasiveness of what William Stringfellow calls the Power of death, in our culture. The second way to understand *Bury the Dead* is through the popular quote often attributed to labor organizer Mother Jones; in the first half of the book we "Pray for the dead," and in the second we "Fight like hell for the living."

The heart of the book is the idea that how Christians respond to death—whether of loved ones or of unnamed collateral damage—is a practical measure of our faith. Life, death, and resurrection are the core of the Christian tradition. But as this collection of writings demonstrates, if we do not engage fully with death and dying, if we hand the sick and the dead off to the professionals, we ignore the incarnate Christ. If we speak Jesus' execution and the miraculous new life of his community as credal formula or religious pass-code, then we miss the point. Nelson Johnson's cry of outrage over Jim Waller's body, Andrea Ferich planting gardens at inner city murder sites, Eda Ruhiye Uca reading biblical conquest narratives, Tom Karlin building a coffin for his infant son, these are stories about how we do death, but they are equally about how we do resurrection.

The process of editing this book has included unexpected gifts and pitfalls. Thankfully few editors face the delicacy of approaching a grieving friend to ask if they are ready to write about their partner's death, or calling about an overdue manuscript on the day of the author's biopsy. And you can't send your edits to the twenty-years-dead for approval, nor chasten them for unreferenced quotations.

As I worked on the index I laughed to discover that that in a book about death, written mostly by Christians, there were so few references to heaven. When Jeff Dietrich and Kieran Prather's contributions arrived in a bundle of yellowing newspapers from the Los Angeles Catholic Worker, they felt like relics—fragile and imbued with the power of the saints. Then at a party I found two of the younger contributors to this volume tucked away in a corner, heads together confiding.

"Working on the article for this death book has put me in a state of crisis."

"Me too!"

As I approached, preparing to offer an appology they continued.

"But it's the best thing I've done in a long time."

"I know, isn't it great!"

In taking on this project, I was seeking a way to put down some of my own grief; instead I found myself carrying the precious stories of others—of their beloved dead and their potent outrage. In Chapter 2, Bill Wylie-Kellermann describes the support his family received from their extended community as, "serial intensive pastoral care." Well, working on this book, sharing stories of grief and tranformation with prophets for companions, became "mutual long-distance technologically-mediated pastoral care." Even more so when, late in the project, my mother was diagnosed with an aggressive and advanced ovarian cancer. As my family navigated hospital coridors and "advanced care planning," blundering into one another in our animal pain, the community of experience, prayer, and support, that this book both calls for and creates, was already assembled and we were held.

So readers, I invite you into that community and into the rest of this book with the words of School of the Americas Watch field organizer, Nico Udu-gama, "Forgetting has always been the tool of the powerful—together we remember." Truly, we re-member, bringing together scattered members as we share our stories of death, resistance and transformation. Amen.

PART I

Death and Burial

1

Learning It in My Bones
Holding Her Body, Touching Nonviolence

Lᴏᴜɪ Wᴏᴏ-Kᴇʟʟᴇʀᴍᴀɴɴ

LʏᴅɪA Wʏʟɪᴇ-Kᴇʟʟᴇʀᴍᴀɴɴ

"Lᴏᴏᴋ ʙᴀᴄᴋ, ᴍᴏᴍ. Yᴏᴜ will never have to see that hospital again."

The biggest smile spread across her face. She had spent the last seven years in and out of hospitals. The wires and beeping almost drove her mad—ripping out IVs and trying to escape her room in the middle of the night. Too often they had to tie her to the bed because her will was so strong—a gift we (almost always) loved about her. We tried to humanize the hospital in those years, reading aloud, singing hymns, knowing the nurses. But it wasn't enough. My mom was always clear that a hospital is no place to live and even more it is no place to die.

So, in September 2005, when we learned that the tumors were back and this time woven in the center of her brain, we knew it was the turning time. We had already decided that we would not do another surgery. When my mom looked back at the hospital, I don't think she was in denial or confused. She knew that this meant she was about to die. She had the miraculous ability to love life and fight with all her being and at the same time hold a freedom to die. I don't know how she did it.

The next four months are a blur of sweet memories. With the knowledge of what was coming each moment was held dear. Our energy and hearts shifted. We released our grasp on hope, no longer trying any treatment we could think of. Now, the work was simply to love one another and be present to the moment. I traveled home from college every weekend during those months. We baked cookies, read books, swam in the Great Lakes, sang together, carved jack-o-lanterns, walked in the woods, watched the snow fall, cuddled, and decorated the Christmas tree. It was an unexpected gift to let go and allow her to die as her body and heart chose.

As the day drew near, our house was filled with people. Community made the coming days possible. We were organized. We had lists and calendars and coordinators covering everything: arranging travel, housing visitors, offering daily prayer, picking Lucy up from high school, and researching the legalities of home wakes and burials. Mindful of the ways that this process would weigh heavy on our family, folks from around the country traveled to Detroit to offer pastoral care for my dad, sister, and me. A whole team of friends and family were assembled to be the "Point of Death Team." When my mom died, they would be ready to take on roles which included carrying her downstairs, washing her body, picking up the dry-ice, making phone calls, and leading liturgy.

The days passed as a slow and beautiful dance of folks coming to say goodbye, offering meals, sharing prayer, sweeping the floor, and keeping watch through the night. During the last seven years, my mom had moved between clarity and confusion, but she always seemed clear and articulate about how she wanted to die. She longed to die at home; to be cremated. No embalming. No funeral home. No hospital.

The night before she died, my sister and I crawled in bed with my mom, her hospital bed right beside the Christmas tree. She no longer spoke or smiled or opened her eyes. We crawled under her arms and felt the skin that had loved us so well through the years. Through the years, we had repeatedly read the C. S. Lewis' Narnia series out loud to one another. That night my dad sat beside us and read the final chapter of the last book:

> And as He spoke He no longer looked to them like a lion; but the things that began to happen after that were so great and beautiful that I cannot write them. And for us this is the end of all the stories, and we can most truly say that they all lived happily ever after. But for them it was only the beginning of the real story. All their life in this world and all their adventures in Narnia had only been the cover and the title page: now at last they were beginning Chapter One of the Great Story, which no one on earth

has read: which goes on for ever: in which every chapter is better than the one before.[1]

My mom believed these words. I often hear her voice run through my head. Years ago, she offered words at a conference about looking forward to and fearing judgment day. She envisioned everyone standing in a circle facing one another. Our sins would be stripped from us—the ones we knew to be sins and then the ones that we didn't know to be sins or pretended not to know. And then we would look around the circle. She anticipated a lot of laughter and maybe some sadness at the ways we had hurt one another. She had such a deep and beautiful belief in heaven. In the final months of my mom's life, I would often ask her how she felt about dying. "I don't know what I want. I love being here with you and Lucy and your dad. But in heaven, I would get to be with my dad and brother and Bill's parents." I was lifted by her words knowing that she wasn't outraged or terrified to die. She had a certainty about heaven and that it was a good and joyful place where all would be together. I yearn for that kind of faith and hold tightly to hers.

The next day, New Year's Eve, life and death wove themselves together making the veil feel very thin. Constant unexpected graces occurred like the casket arriving that very morning, beautifully crafted by friends. They had started building it seven years earlier when they first heard of her diagnosis. It sat in their basement unfinished for years. Another friend sewed a lovely and strong blanket with handles that could be used to carry her body downstairs. The Point of Death Team gathered for a meeting that morning to run through how each step would go.

In the afternoon, my sister and I left for massages we had received as gifts. I kissed my mom on the forehead and whispered to her how much I loved her. I was confident she still had a few more days to live, but every time I left the house I ran the risk. For weeks, I had been voicing all my love and gratitude out loud over and over again just in case it was goodbye.

While we were out, we got the news. I had imagined and prepared for this moment since I was twelve years old, but I had never actually expected to hear—she's dead. I hung up stunned and repeated the two stark words aloud to my sister and friends. Silence. Lucy began to cry. Suddenly, we were all sobbing. We sped home with nothing but the sound of tears and gasps guiding our way. How did this happen? How could I not have been there? Rage and grief.

1. C. S. Lewis, *The Last Battle* (1956; reprinted, New York: Collier, 1975), 183–84.

Part I: Death and Burial

I jumped out of the still-moving car and ran the steps three at a time. At the top of the stairs, my mom's body was sitting in a chair ready to be carried downstairs. I fell upon her. Lucy right behind me. We wailed. She was still warm. I couldn't let go. Holding her so close as if to take her warmth as my own. I sat on her lap for the last time and wept. Family and community stood around crying and giving us this space. Daughters saying goodbye to their mother.

She was carried downstairs and laid out on the table. The women of the community gathered around her. Sage and sweetgrass burned. Taizé chants filled the space. I traced her eyes and nose—committing them to memory. I washed her hair and felt the history of the years—scars and wounds. Each line and bone shift a memory of a brain surgery. Her face was cleansed by my tears. Slowly, the warmth was leaving her. I soaked it in. None of us had ever done this before, but it came smoothly and beautifully as if we had never forgotten our ancestors' movements.

We laid her in the casket, dry ice below her. Lucy had picked out her outfit including the bright red hat we'd given her for Christmas a year ago. The house began to fill. Singing. Stories. Weeping. Prayer. Laughter. Embrace. It went on like this for days. Her body remained with us, never alone, honored with love. After three days, my dad accompanied her body and pushed the casket in to be cremated.

Looking back on those days, I am overwhelmed with gratitude. For the memory of her warmth on my hands and her cheek against mine. For being able to hold and say goodbye to her body. For knowing that she was never alone. For being held by a community. I am grateful for the ordinary moments turned sacrament, for a learning that went right to my bones, and to know she went home by another way.

I know that all of this is far from the usual path. In the United States, bodies are handled by hospitals and funeral homes. It has all become privatized and professionalized—removed from our parlors and our hands. Death is masked behind closed doors and makeup. Bodies are filled with chemicals and locked in indestructible boxes. The natural processes, ancient wisdom, and relationship with the earth completely removed.

The costs of these recent practices are serious. We have lost control of the rituals around dying while our culture is plagued with and perpetuating death around us. I am mindful of the young people shot and killed due to racial profiling, of the suicides of gay teens. In my own neighborhood, I ache with the children whose fathers died trying to cross the Mexican desert to reconnect with their families. Then there are the endless wars fought with drones and weapons of mass destruction murdering hundreds of thousands. Death is everywhere. Yet we are removed from the process of touching, holding, and crying over the bodies.

Instead of grief, there is numbness, blindness, fear, ignorance, and silence. We have pushed death away. Struggling to make it invisible. Paying money to keep the pain from our hearts. What happens if we forget how to grieve together?

Being raised in the Detroit Catholic Worker Community, nonviolence was woven into the fabric of my childhood. But it became permanent on my heart and future in high school when the second plane hit the twin towers during choir class sophomore year. I listened as the language of grief and anger was so quickly manipulated to justify a war on terror. I watched as we responded with bombs in Afghanistan and then with Shock and Awe in Iraq. My heart broke. I jumped on every bus to New York and DC I could find, putting my feet with my heart. No longer just because that was how I was raised, but because I felt the urgent need within myself. The need to say no with everything I had. Pleading to stop killing any more human beings. I could not comprehend our willingness to kill so easily.

At home, my mom was dying. I lived with a constant ache within me. Every day a gift. Every tomorrow unknown. I felt so strongly what the loss of my mother would mean. I watched how many people her life impacted. And she was just one person. How could I wish this on anyone? How could causing someone this much pain be a solution to any problem? What right did we have to take another life? I could no longer try to reason or make sense of government-sponsored violence. It is absurd and despicable!

Grief is a powerful force. Mourning the dead is a shared human experience. It is an act of community whether you gather in a home, lift a glass, picnic in the graveyards, wash the body, or carry the casket down the road led by trombones. The transformative power of grief is something the powers that be have always known. In every age, empires have hidden death, refusing the rituals around the bodies, and working to systematically deny communities the right to grieve.

While I was in college, George W. Bush forbid the media to show images of caskets coming home from Afghanistan and Iraq. He was invested in hiding the reality of death from the eyes of the country. It was easy to go about my day without ever thinking about the wars.

Towards the end of college, my partner and I were on an immersion trip to Taizé, France. The only other group with us for the week, were Christian Palestinian university students. We spent the week sharing meals, work, and prayer. They shared with us about their lives under occupation; they looked us in the eyes and said, "Your country is funding this occupation." At home, we realized we needed to learn more and actively work against the occupation. We joined Michigan Peace Team on a month-long delegation to the West Bank that was focused on nonviolent intervention. During that time, we traveled to the places where Palestinians had asked for an international presence. We accompanied shepherds who had been attacked by settlers, slept in orphanages that had been raided by the Israeli military, documented abuses at check points, and stood alongside folks in nonviolent protests along the wall.

While we were there, a seventeen-year-old Palestinian was shot dead by the Israeli army while he painted a neighbor's house. The community gathered and hundreds carried the casket through the streets to the cemetery, only to be met at the entrance by the Israeli military. They fired on the crowd for hours until everyone was forced to return home. I felt outrage. Refusing to allow a community the rituals around death is cruel and violating.

How powerful the grieving of community must be. Being kept numb and afraid is good for our foreign policy, war profiteering, and domination.

Grief becomes an act of resistance—to stand before empire, before the face of death, and pour out our love and our tears. It's no coincidence that blessed are those who mourn ranks up with those who hunger and thirst for justice, show mercy, and are peacemakers. It is work we are called to do. A gospel mandate. Mourn in the face of empire. Resist a culture of death.

What would happen if as a country we grieved together? If we mourned every soldier who died, every grandmother killed in Iraq, every prisoner executed on death row, every homeless person who dies in our own neighborhoods? Could we keep going? Could we keep using our money to participate in it?

Every year, thousands gather at the School of the Americas[2] and raise crosses and sing ¡Presente! as names are sung for hours—all victims of those trained at the SOA. At the foot of the White House, people lay

2. The School of the Americas, now called Western Hemisphere Institute for Security Cooperation, is a US Defense Department training school in Fort Benning, Georgia for Latin American military. There are numerous documented cases of SOA/WHISC graduates involved human rights violations, including kidnapping, torture, and murder. Online: www.soaw.org/.

caskets by the fence and read the names of those erased as "collateral damage" in Iraq and Afghanistan. In Palestine, communities bury their dead even when it means more imprisonment and violence. In the Old Testament, Rizpah disobeys the king to care for the bodies of her dead sons (2 Sam 21:8–13). Tobit breaks the law by performing burials for enemies and outcasts (Tobit 1:17—2:8). We join this ancient struggle by bringing our grief into the open, proclaiming it publicly, joining the cries, no matter the risk or cost. We also resist the culture of death, by the simple candles we light in our own homes, by pilgrimaging to the burial sites, and by remembering and telling the stories.

Nestled in a grove of pine trees, a candle-lit lamppost is the only marker of my mom's ashes given back to the earth. Kids have wandered into the woods believing they have discovered Narnia. It is the light that shines amidst a world cursed to always be winter and never Christmas.

This is the place that I pilgrimage to. Sitting alone in the woods missing her love and life around me. We buried her ashes on Easter day, perhaps a liturgical oddity, but she was a true witness to the way that death and resurrection are bound together.

In the years leading to her death, she often talked about her intention to die with her eyes open and spirit willing. In no way was it easy, but she truly found within her a freedom to die. I watched the way that freedom to die became a freedom to live. She had a boundless spirit filled with awe for the mystery of life.

To resist the culture of death around us, we do go to the places of sorrow weeping, but we cannot help but rise dancing.

I witnessed this transformation at a protest in the village of Saara in the West Bank. A roadblock had been dumped by the Israeli military on the main road leaving town. This enormous pile of dirt blocked the people from getting to work, hospitals, and extended family. The town began holding weekly, nonviolent protests. I marched alongside two hundred people bearing signs and chanting out choruses of justice and nonviolence. They carried shovels to symbolically begin to remove the dirt. It was a beautiful sight. Perhaps most amazing of all, was that the majority of the people were children between the ages of five and fifteen.

We arrived at the roadblock and were immediately met by eight military vehicles and snipers climbing the hills ready to shoot at anytime. Chants rang. Shovels dug at the earth. Sound bombs fired. Tear gas spread. People fled. Children ran for their lives.

We gathered back in the center of town; no one was injured; I thought it was over. But quickly, consensus was reached to go back to the roadblock. We marched back slowly. After negotiation between the parents and soldiers, the soldiers shouted that we had seven minutes before they would begin to open fire. At that moment, four boys came forward in traditional Palestinian dress. They stood in front of the roadblock, just feet in front of the military vehicles. And they began to dance the Dabka, the traditional Palestinian dance. The air changed from fear and anger to joy and celebration. Everyone began to clap and sing and shout for joy. It was a courageous and powerful seven minutes.

Resurrection. To go to the places of death and injustice exposing the truth. To stand before the face of death mindful of the risks and cost. To honor the grief and anger. And then to dance. To choose life and freedom. It is a dance that has been going on for a very long time. It is a dance that we are all invited to join.

> Very early on Sunday morning, the women went to the tomb, carrying spices they had prepared. They found the stone rolled away from the entrance to the tomb, so they went in, but they did not find the body of the Jesus. (Luke 24:1–3)

After Jesus was killed, the disciples ran in fear. Yet there were those who refused to be afraid. It was the women. In the face of deep pain and loss, they went to the tomb carrying their local herbs to care for the body. I can almost catch the smell in the breeze like sweetgrass and sage in my own region and time. It was no small journey to go to the tomb that was closed, sealed, and guarded by the authorities.

The women in the Gospel did not go looking for resurrection. They were looking for death. They traveled to mourn the dead, to seek out the injustice, to be in solidarity, to feel the pain, to be community, to look death in the face, and to resist fear. It is while grieving and honoring the dead that the women witnessed the Resurrection.

These women call us to go to the places of suffering and death in our world. If we believe and celebrate the Resurrection, it is indeed a call to action. Where are we mourning? What death has our culture ignored? Or become numb to? What death have we been afraid to face? Let us weep in Baghdad, on our streets, outside our prisons, on the borders, at the foot of the White House, at the headquarters of Halliburton, in the homes of the Palestinians, and in our own living rooms. Then maybe, amidst the tears for the death and killing of our brothers and sisters, we too might stumble upon the Resurrection.

2

Dying in Community
Freedom and Decision[1]

BILL WYLIE-KELLERMANN

GETHSEMANE

CAREFULLY TESTING THE STEPS, and helping one another over the missing slats of stair, Jeanie Wylie and I climbed the weather-worn frame of the fire watchtower. It was February 1982, but the Kentucky hills were warm in the winter sun. A church bell called the start of the noon office. Pushing up and through the trap door we suddenly had a view of the Abby below where the monks of Gethsemane were lifting the Psalms in Gregorian and interceding for us all. Thomas Merton had once requested this abandoned look out for a hermitage, but the abbot put him off.

"So, are we here to decide something?" she asked, a rhetorical question. Our hands touched on the rusting metal ledge. I had spent a month with the monks ostensibly weighing a choice, which was really a done deal when I arrived. Since I'd hitchhiked from Detroit, she had driven down to pick me up, bearing at my request two leather shoe thongs. They were for stringing each of us a single bead of a fossil, actually a reed segment from the days this bioregion was lush with wetland grass. These

1. This article is excerpted from Bill Wylie-Kellermann's forthcoming book *Dying Humanly: The Resurrected Life of Jeanie Wylie-Kellermann*.

11

two had been dredged from a streambed and spread with the gravel of the monastery's farm lanes. I'd found them in my walking meditations through the hills. They would be for us engagement rings.

"Yes," I replied, pulling out the lanyard and placing it round her neck. I gave her the other and she did the same to me. We kissed and lingered in the holding, then turned back toward the view. So close we could nearly have touched it, a hawk hovered before us on the rolling-gunderneath him steady air.

The decision to marry Jeanie Wylie was the easiest I'd ever made. I just knew it, "balls to bones." Or better, we knew it together. From the earliest conversations she and I understood this commitment to mean working out our salvation within the vocation of marriage. I suppose I am still working it out, even with these words.

COMMUNAL DISCERNMENT

When Jeanie was struck down in September of 1998 with a most aggressive brain tumor, medical decision-making became a constant. There was a young resident at the first hospitalization who was privy to the passing along of the diagnosis. He also looked us in the eye and offered advice, "Don't be buffaloed. Think quality of life. It's going to be an issue." He would be shocked, I'm certain, to discover the length of Jeanie's survival—seven and a half years, some of the decisions we made, and even in the end how we understood quality of life. But it was a rare moment, an official of the medical system urging on us our own freedom. That stuck.

Clinical trials, alternative therapies, never mind the standards of chemo and radiation. All have invisible pressures behind them. Doctors commending clinical trials are not offering disinterested advice; they are also invested researchers tending not just a project but a career. Hospitals are capitalized heavily into radiation devices they need to pay for by billing your insurance company. Alternative therapies make big claims, often selling themselves without the benefit of independent testing or analysis. Keeping your feet means dragging them sometimes and kicking with them at others. Or even just turning on your heel and walking out the room. Anyway here's where community was such a help in our experience.

We were blessed to have what we variously called the clearness committee or query circle or discernment group. Formally, a clearness committee is a Quaker thing. There are pamphlets on how to form and run one: a little strict with a clerk and a process basically composed of questions. The idea is that the group doesn't insert itself with advice but poses probing questions to those who seek clarity—toward bringing their own inner leadings into the light. We began with this process, though it quickly morphed informal. It was a prayerful circle, generally convened in silence with a candle or concluding with prayer. Jeanie was always part of it, and often my daughter Lydia. The others were members of our community both near and far.

Their role varied over time. Jeanie and I did ask them for advice periodically, and they freely gave. They would sometimes help us sort the issues so we could make a kind of decision tree. When we knew what we wanted or needed to do, but felt the life and death gravity of it, they would confirm the choice and agree to bear the burden of the decision. We were in this together. This group helped organize anniversary events and birthday celebrations. They offered resources—like pursuing legal or medical information. They scheduled community care-giving for Jeanie when I was out of town. They stood ready to raise funds if need be. We asked of them way more than thinking up deft questions. In general, they were the constant presence of community to our healing and dying. They were the seed of what would eventually become a "hospice community."

We outright resisted the immediate pressures of conventional radiation/chemo (with pretty thin advantage to commend them, but tons of institutional momentum). Jeanie took an early lead in reading over and thinking through alternative treatments. At a certain point friends of ours subscribed us to an online service that summarized and independently evaluated various strange and emerging options. Everything from crystals to vaccines made from urine, to electrical devices designed to kill "the parasites that cause cancer," were closely considered. Please don't laugh. Hidden among its weirder cures, we found both the alternatives that got us through seven years of life.

Probably the hardest judgment call we made involved radiation after a second tumor surgery. Jeanie Wylie was pretty dead set against radiation. When that was being pressed upon us once again, she declared herself freely and fully prepared to die. I remember sitting in the car along the side of a quiet dirt road. We prayed together and decided to just let the course of things play out. It was in a way the first choosing for hospice. But then I couldn't sleep. Or eat. A rock formed in my gut. I reopened the decision process and made the case for reversal. And she assented. Jesus. It's the one choice I work hard not to regret. In part because the initiative was so categorically mine. Radiation has long-term consequences presumed to be a moot point in her expected timeline. But then she stuck around for the longer haul. I always wondered quietly how many of her late deficits were related to radiation necrosis rather than tumor growth. We'll never know and I just prayed to let it go.

There is confession in that. I aspired to the freedom already named, but grasped it unevenly and only in part. And yet, decision by decision, in the mysteries of providence, and borne by community, we went forward.

It needs be said too, that we went through this ordeal "privileged" to draw on financial support from friends as well as the options of quality church-based insurance. These are to be sure a feature of "life in community" in some broad sense. But when one in six people in this country have neither health insurance nor friends of means, we can't be blinded to the privilege entailed. An account of this same illness told by one of our neighbors down the block might also be about the graces of dying well, but I wager the story would be shorter and more painful.

MESSAGE IN A PLASTIC BAG

In the last months of 2005, cleaning house for the pending final hospitality, I came upon something in a stack of papers I might easily have tossed—several hand-written post-it notes in a little plastic bag. The pages were carefully numbered and the penciled instructions were in Jeanie's hand. It had been written the year prior and she must have carried it on her person, or maybe in the medical bag, with an eye toward final contingencies.

> To anyone who finds this:
> Lucy just started h.s. She's vibrant (taking 5 dance classes on M & W), sings in plays—nice pitch—and gets straight A's Cell # xxx-xxx-xxxx
> Lydia has a cell phone too and because she's extremely responsible, she's—of the 3 W-K's—most likely to have it on and she's a good sleuth. (She'd be most able to track Lucy down—unless she went home with a new friend from school.) She'd also apply herself to finding Bill. (In finding people, she's as capable as me.) Her cell # is xxx-xxx-xxxx. I was planning on having all our cell #s end

in 1967, Year of Detroit's big rebellion. But Bill got Lucy's phone and they assigned her the first available number.

At present, I'm the only one without a cell phone and without a computer of my own. Bill promised me one as a birthday gift (contingent on my clearing space for it. Never mind that he has a study upstairs you can't even move in without stepping on something of value.) His cell # is xxx-xxx-xxxx. Like Lydia his first response would be to come home. I'd be really glad to see all 3 (as long as I can recognize them). The last thing my kids need is for me to smile and say "and who are these lovely girls." (Your Mom is practically required to know you.) so make sure someone is present to interpret. 1) Any time you notice that I have more context than they've been provided—point it out. 2) Any time you see that I care for them—point it out. 3) If it seems I have a sense of who is living with me point that out too.

I laughed and I cried. I am so busted by that. The cell phones, which I had long resisted, were a concession to medical emergency and the persistence of my road-work. The birthday thing is true; she couldn't be trusted alone on my laptop without navigating her curiosity into software settings or some such damage and I never delivered on my intent to arrange her something else. A true regret. (After the note surfaced and I addressed it, she did forgive me that). And my attic study truly is an untraversable mess, to which I forbid guided tours. But I wept to read it as well. For the love and care she was taking with the girls, even me. And for her imagining an end she would need to self-manage among strangers in a hospital or nursing home. I'm so glad we all conspired to make that end different, even sacred and beautiful, though God knows, she self-managed a good bit of it anyway.

HOSPICE: INSTITUTION OR COMMUNITY

I know there is gut and grace, perhaps in equal measure, both in healing and in dying, but the decision to quit treatment and die well is still an extraordinary event of inner turning. Or so it was for us. Moreover, it was only complicated by the emotional contradictions which accompany the traversing of such terrain. In the long haul fight, I confess a weary inner voice, largely secret and suppressed, which periodically whispered, Couldn't it just be over? Or, like Lydia, How many more miracles can we bear? Suddenly that voice seemed to have been given its reign in the dying time. But now with its wish all but fulfilled, I grasped at precious moments and might have clung to life by my fingernails if I could but hold it—all the while letting go. Grace upon grace means being granted (and granting ourselves) the permission to be in the turmoils of such contradiction.

Hospice was waiting us in the wings, but to get there meant setting aside certain medical options. One was an oral chemo, generally well-tolerated, with side effects easy to control which might grant some additional time. Sounds good, no? Yes, but . . . the odds were short that it would work and above all, it would tie us to a rigid out-patient regimen of weekly blood tests and scans to monitor the dosage and then submission to hospitalization if adjustments were needed. With the discernment circle at the dining room table, I remember my inner sigh, when we decided to forego it.

Hospice, and perhaps especially the hospice care movement in North America, stakes a claim for dying well. By no means do I mean to imply that hospice and dying well are synonymous. Jesus, for example, died well in excruciating torture. An assassin's bullet, an absurd car wreck, or a frantic hospital effort to save and survive—none of these preclude dying well in my understanding. I try to imagine the latter, scrambling mightily in a heroic fight with all the medical resources in hand and watching a life slip away; that would surely make for a different variety of grief, at least initially. The movement for hospice, however, conscientiously reclaims the intent of dying well with care.

By conventional definition, hospice involves non-interventive, palliative care, simply making the person as comfortable, and aware, as possible while she dies. She is treated as a person approaching death rather than a patient. Hospice reclaims space for dying, takes it back from the more exposed and invasive locations of American medical care. It opens the possibility, at home or in a more comfortable facility, of making beauty, of re-creating sacred space. It involves an act of freedom, reasserting personal control of decision-making, unhooking from the grip of the medical regime. It opens the way for family and community and friendship to become primary. Relationships and the inner life of the dying, take pride of place over any of the ordinary distractions.

And yet, hospice, to be made more widely accessible, has become less community or movement than institution. It is these days supported, if not encouraged, and fully funded by the insurance industry because people effectively opt out of expensive procedures and last ditch heroics. They do retain a freedom to change their minds, but that's regulated by a series of protocols and limitations. Hospice programs are rich in caring professionals, but commercial necessities assert a client-based approach even where they move beyond medical to social or even pastoral care. From the perspective of Jeanie's deathbed, I would say that a hospice program best supports and enables a real hospice community to gather round. The care we got was more than adequate, from a number of kind and competent folks. They taught things we needed, but I'm comforted to believe we could have done it well, even without them. As poor folk with naught but extended families regularly do.

SERIAL INTENSIVE PASTORAL CARE

When we'd made the decision for hospice, our family four also had a conversation about pastoral care for our family. In this home stretch, on whom did we want to be leaning? From our worshiping communities, we had two obvious choices, much beloved. One was a thorough extrovert, thinking aloud, filling a room, aggressive and inventive in a crisis, diving in with both feet to move institutions or remedy situations. The other was a compleat introvert, the epitome of contemplative nonattachment, but fully present in a kind of Zen silence. Hmmm. The girls shook their heads and thought. Long. And nothing was resolved just then.

A number of dear friends from around the country, who'd been sharing the journey with us from the beginning, took counsel together and tried to organize a gathering at our place, which complex schedules and short time precluded. In lieu of that, we calendared in a series of weekend visitations. We didn't realize it at the time, but we were in effect stumbling upon a new pastoral model. Let me christen it—serial intensive pastoral care.

First in the series came social justice activist and writer, and more to the point, longstanding friend, Joyce Hollyday, who co-pastors a new congregation in Asheville, North Carolina. She joined us bearing gifts for an invented family holiday. Her most notable gift however, was her care pastorally. She made time to get a walk and a talk with everyone, including Jeanie, probing with questions the state of each heart. Then her last evening we gathered around for a family conversation which she facilitated. We talked freely, but she knew where all the hidden cards were waiting and needing to be laid on the table. It was good.

ORGANIZING THE WAY HOME

Next Ched Myers and Elaine Enns flew themselves in from California. They had several years prior been primaries in the hospice community around the Guadalupe Catholic Worker which surrounded our common friend Ladon in his crossing over. So they brought tested wisdom about ways to order such a community. They knew how to make everyone a part as helpers and workers rather than mere guests. While tending our hearts, they effectively offered a short course in pastoral administration for the dying time. Ched and Elaine knew about ducking the mortuary system, about homemade coffins, how to get dry ice and what parts of the body require it most. They brought a wealth of community wisdom, a common store for which we yearned without even knowing.

At their counsel we contracted a dear friend, Simone Sagovac, a gifted labor and environmental organizer, to organize us. As the days intensified I felt myself center and open. I was at my best, fully alert, mindful of my own heart, but attentive to others and the dynamics of the scene. Having an organizer meant I could consult, and to an extent help direct the process, without be whelmed over by logistics. It was a rare gift, not to be presumed. Carpentry would happen around us: widening doorspaces, a ramp was constructed on the front lawn to slide the casket out the front window (what must the neighbors have thought?). Prayer groups arrived with psalms and instruments in hand. Airport runs would be coordinated and meals rewarmed in casserole dishes. We were being borne in a facilitated community.

ALL MORTAL FLESH

Jeanie's altar, where her ashes rested from Epiphany to Easter, stands behind me as I write. It is like a Dia de los Muertos *ofrenda*, dense with sacramentals: a basket where she ritually deposited her hospital wrist bands, a wooden bowl of collected stones, effigies of herself fabricated from natural and found materials, family photos and icons, candles, woven crosses, a score of angels. A late addition was Jeanie's last drawing, a Christmas present for me. It's a provocative intrigue: We are facing one another, me unaccountably skinny and naked, she in a dress with her back to view—possibly bowing shyly but more likely lifting her skirt and strutting her stuff. It calls to mind our lovemaking—as it seems verily designed to do. I wish I could recall in specificity the last time we did so. It is best, I imagine, always to make love as though it could be the last.

There actually is an ethic of sorts in that approach. The simplest way to frame the ethical version is to ask: Would I be content for this to be my last act? Would I be willing to be transported suddenly and finally to the presence of God's judgment and mercy, while I am engaged in this word or deed? It clarifies the mind in a very concrete way. Of course there are heroic doings and grand gestures that appeal readily to this ethic. But there are also simple and ordinary ones. My Mom collapsed while gardening in the retirement village. She'd have been content, and surely was. Not, notice, would she choose this way, but would she be content? I might not want to die in car crash, but where was I headed and on whose behalf? Routes or actions which give us pause might want to be rethought. One could name this an "eschatological" ethic—the moral content of "last things." Or, just as simply, an ethic of dying well.

Anyway, as to lovemaking, I'm saddened not to have a precise memory. At a certain point she just began declining my bedroom advances, though never my tender affections. That ought to have made an impression since it was so rare—in fact, she with equal ardor would as often initiate. But then, her demure become persistent. It could certainly have been a simple body thing, the gradual shutting down of the drive along with other systems. Each reluctance seemed fair at the time, or natural, since she had a right to feel weary or in pain, but now I wonder if it weren't a kind of decision unannounced. Was she beginning a deliberate process of disconnecting from her own body of desires? Slowly trimming the lamp. Banking the inner coals. Was she saving the two of us the great final wrench from each others' arms? Protecting me in some sense? I don't know. The Christmas drawing is a playful tease. Perhaps not having, in memory, the one "last time," makes all the times equally penultimate in a wild and vivid joy. Even now in bodily memory I conform myself in the night to where she's not, and smile or cry.

Here the poem I rose to write for her that Christmas morning:

Let All Mortal

Because the Word takes flesh
we wreathe winterlight with candles,

Part I: Death and Burial

make feast and sing
to story the stable
where end and beginning
flesh from flesh
are one frail body, even divine.

Once in a jail cell
waiting out another Advent
I harbored arcane joys
by summoning in memory and anticipation
every inch of your sweet flesh
by candlelight kissed and caressed;
such enough is an ache
on which a body may thrive or survive.

How many times before and since
have I breathed your breath
or fit dreaming beside you?
Even now I rise from a dream's breath
to write.

Your belly is marked
with the rivulet stretches of child born spending
flesh of your flesh of our flesh
pushed and pulled 'til
breaking the light of this world,
those two.

I think of others unmet
flesh still too soon
witnessed in roots or branches of
this or that apple tree's grief.

Now your flesh is marked
with the surgeon's knife
chasing the intruder
whose death grip
pretends dominion in you.
But no.
Not in your wounded head
let alone your great heart.
Not today. Not ever. Not in the end.
That nor this.

God you were strong
though by muscle or pure will
I could never be certain,

but to be the one in your grip
squeezed as never to let go -
I could hurt with that joy
forever.

What among the griefs
to watch the ebbing of that power,
grace supplanting will
by necessity and choice.

I do know the weight of your flesh,
hefting it upright
these days again and again
overriding my own back's focused complaint.
How many more times will you resist the pull of earth
to walk your will upon the stairs?

And still this morning
I kiss your hands and lips
surrogate for everywhere and always,
this body of earth
filled with the glory of God
and the dwelling of the straw strewn Word

All flesh
with your sweet body
shall see it together.

The following day, Feast of Stephen, my brothers and their families came for dinner and gifts. When Jeanie took to bed that afternoon it was really for the last time. Without spreading any sense of urgency, the hospice nurse allowed that it was time for the delivery of the hospital bed, which seemed to appear with an unobtrusive quiet, almost immediately beside the Christmas tree. But I did want one last night in our own bed and clung to her, dampening that worn flannel gown with tears in the dark.

TIME TO CROSS

We were blessed by the prodding discernment and instinct of beloved Simone. She was doggedly organizing the "point of death team"—folks who had volunteered to hurry to the scene when Jeanie died. Ordinarily, at the moment of death, families and their grief communities are immediately separated from the body of their beloved, disempowered in their decision-making, and alienated from the traditional community rites of passage. The sacred body of the dead is legally regulated, and by those regulations assaulted, physically and chemically. Burial is controlled more by commercial forces than by health concerns and is, in fact, counter to any real organic cycle. The process of grieving is likewise commodified. Pastoral care is limited and reframed by social and economic forces not of the faith community's making. But it would not be so among us.

We could avoid the undertaker, but not rigor mortis, so we needed a disciplined readiness to act quickly, moving her to the downstairs flat where the wake would take place, preparing her body and positioning it in the coffin. Simone came prepared with handouts. Lists of responsibilities, but also details of the changes a body goes through, quite frank about the untoward messiness possible.

On a similar impulse, my brother Steve and his wife Carol were dispatched to fetch the coffin lovingly made in Milwaukee. It arrived in time for trial runs, but even more it served to ritualize this practical communion of necessity and grace. We were ready.

In the afternoon Lydia and Lucy went off for massages as they had been gifted, while my brothers and in-law sisters vigiled with me at bedside. And then it came. Quicker than we guessed. Jeanie's breathing was belabored as the fluid in her chest increased. My concern was growing, and it seemed like the girls ought to have been done and on their way back. I called Lydia's cell and got voicemail, but left a careful message urging them to hurry home, that Mom's time seemed to be upon us, and that I loved them both so much. The time was indeed upon us. I held Jeanie and spoke love to her. My brothers were close. We were one in hands and tears. When she took her final breath and crossed over, I prayed for us all. Thanks be to God. Jeanie is.

We sat in silence for a bit. I called her Mom. I phoned Simone and set things in motion.

Now the hard thing. Lydia called in. Without thinking, I assumed she was responding to my urgent phone message. She wasn't. The exchange remains sharp in both our memories. I want to make allowance for myself being in shock, but it wasn't a time for the luxury of shock.

Me: "Hey."
Lydia: "Hello."
Me: "Mom's dead."
Lydia: "What?"
Me: "Mom died, Sweetie."
Silence

Me: "You there?"

Lydia: "Yeah, uh when?"

Me: "About ten minutes ago."

Silence

Lydia: "Ok, on our way."

Hanging up, to Lucy: "Mom's dead."

The countering grace is that this transpired as they stood among their closest friends in community, kids they had known since the birth of each. And further that they were driven home in shared tears by these very friends.

DEAD WEIGHT

Meanwhile, I surely was a bit beclouded. Although the point of death team was on the way, a number of them from homes right on the block, I was feeling the urgency to move Jeanie's body. We had planned to use the Amish oak armchair to carry her down the front hall stairs, as it was much easier to navigate around corner landings than any sort of stretcher we then had available. The chair was there by the bed, and in my state, it seemed to me a simple maneuver that brother Paul and I could hoist her into it. I'm thinkin' heck, I'm accustomed even to getting her up off the floor when required. If we sat her up, swung her feet round, and then lifted her in one smooth motion it ought to work.

You know? there really is a thing called dead weight. And Jeanie had become it. She was not in a position to help us in the least. As we made the one smooth motion, the reality suddenly dawned on us as she began to slip toward the floor. Near at hand, my sister-in-law Pat, a small but athletic high school Phys Ed teacher, stepped into the breach. She was not about to let Jeanie suffer this indignity. Paul and I were practically forced to stand back as she wrapped her arms around Jeanie's torso, all the while breathing, "No baby. No. You are *not* going down." And with a single irresistible lift set her in the chair.

KEENING LIKE EUCHARISTIC PRAYERS

Slumped, but upright, Jeanie sat enthroned. We had bought the chair with firm wooden arms for the latter living days so she could help lift herself up and out. Now they held her in. We fixed her eyes closed and jaw shut, as well advised, and tied her jaw firmly in place with a scarf. The point of death team, and others on the block who'd gotten word, were trickling in and gathering round beginning to think logistics for the move downstairs when the girls arrived. They fell on her at once and began an unrestrained wail, near keening. Each of their godmothers were present and able to touch them, but apart from that everyone stood back and let them voice their pain, and in it the grief of community. The whole group was fully focused, completely present, almost as though we were transfixed in a common mystical experience. Looking back, I wonder if the depth of that shared moment came because something similar was rehearsed among us each week at the community eucharist, in the body lifted—another mystery beheld in common.

For whatever the time it might have been, I stood back myself and allowed their cries to be my own. But when I knew it to be right, I came close and began, one at a time, whispering in their ears, calling them back into the room, back to themselves. Lucy was the harder pull, finally having to be lifted and commended to other arms, so logistics could again assert themselves. But all that involved pulling myself from bereaved partner to loving parent (and eventually clouded logician).

EXTREME SMUDGE AND THE BOUNCE

As we prepared again to move, I had the presence of mind to mark the moment with a "smudge," igniting in a bowl a bundle of California sage. A big bundle. Immediately left unattended, it would burn potently of its own accord.

Meanwhile, the tied scarf was proving inadequate to its task. As we carried her body down the winding stairwell I noticed that her mouth was opening. Her lips formed a perfect "Oh" as if she were some belated caroler echoing the angels' Gloria. I thought: this bodes ill for a casket pose. Was this the first sign of being in over our heads in handling the body ourselves?

In the downstairs dining room, things were coming together. The cooling board, an unused door from the basement was leveled with biblical commentaries. We positioned the chair and discussed the maneuver of hefting her body to board. Beneath my locked fingers I cradled her head lovingly and felt the ache in my chest. On a count we lifted and swung her over to the board, but as we reached the spot our coordination went out of sync. I felt her sweet head slip from my hands. As I uttered, "Oh, no!" her head took a small bounce on the table, her jaw snapped shut as if by design, forming her lips into a subtle smile worthy of DaVinci's brush.

Thereupon the women took up tasks with the ritual assurance of some deep memory recovered in the doing. There were in their number a couple of nurses who brought a certain experience, but this was a first to both of them. An Immaculate Heart of Mary sister who had been privy to deaths at the motherhouse brought cotton balls and knew the places they were needed. Certainly Simone's frank instructions about what to expect cleared the air of some anxieties, but it seemed these women just knew in their hands and their bones what it meant to treat these practicalities with love, with a sacred deliberance.

The men took to instinctive helps as well. The hospital bed and medical accouterments were dismantled and carried off to the basement, returning the living space immediately to its more regular hospitable use. They rehung doors which had been removed for wheel chair or medical access. While the downstairs flat was being sanctified, the upstairs was normalized.

When it came time to move her body to the casket, the intuitive gender division resolved and the lift was shared. The casket was a perfect fit. The dry ice, timely at hand, was packed with ease into a special compartment under an insulated blanket. Jeanie was in state.

Meanwhile in addition to the point of death team who had been called, the group joining prayer for the evening's bedside vigil began to arrive. A big group. And the smudge unattended was making its purifying presence densely known. When the hospice nurse arrived to arrange the death certificate and reclaim by count any remaining morphine patches, her eyes reflected a degree of panic: there were sixty people in a house full of smoke and Latin chants. This was not your ordinary hospice situation.

Josie Winterfeld of Jubilee Partners in Georgia had arrived earlier that day anticipating a weekend of pastoral care with us. She came prepared to lead prayer that evening at Jeanie's bedside, but now it was coffinside—we gathered around the body. Her touch was simple, poetic, deep—just what the moment required. Another arrival in the grace of time. That evening, in a tradition taken from her own Russian Orthodox roots, our neighbor Martha sat down by candlelight to read in its entirety the Psalter over Jeanie's estated body.

At the wake our pastors, the extrovert organizer and the catholic Zen master, presided. There is a nice photo of me touching Jeanie's face with tenderness. Tears are running down my cheeks, but my face is slightly contorted with a chortle of laughter.

I presided for the last event myself, closing the oaken casket as the final in a rich series, wearing the embroidered stole itself a gift from Jeanie. Lydia placed in her mother's hand Jeanie's original paperback of *The Lion, The Witch, and the Wardrobe*. After silence and song, we removed the ice, sealed the box, rolled it to the window and out.

Jeanie had been firm on cremation. The journey to the crematorium was a family thing—mostly my brothers and spouses. Once again we would see what's conventionally hidden. We must have seemed the oddity. I'm sure the workers were unaccustomed to people pulling up in a minivan to deliver bodies themselves, though they were awkwardly gracious. One of them sketched me the dimensions of the ashes container on the back of a yellow order form. The place was a small industrial operation. We backed round to a docking door and, like thoroughly functional pallbearers, bore our burden inside to the furnace, hoisting her sweet remains into the mouth of the great iron device. It seemed our ceremonialism was exhausted. No circle. No prayer aloud. The final push into the burner was its own spare and complete act. The simplest of lettings go. And the door rolling down was amen.

3

My Near-Death Experience
Reassessing the Morality of Mortality

Joyce Hollyday

Leftover scraps of holiday music filter into my mother's small room through the TV mounted on the wall, as 2011 slowly creeps up on us. She's snoring lightly. I'm in the recliner by her bed, putting finishing touches on a baby blanket I'm crocheting for my nephew's daughter, expected to arrive at any moment—the great-granddaughter my mother will never meet.

I'm here for a few hours to ring in the New Year with Mom, making up for the fact that a blinding blizzard kept me away from her on Christmas Day. She doesn't know that I missed Christmas any more than she knows that this is New Year's Eve, but I feel better being here. When my sisters and I were children, she always brought out the fancy crystal goblets etched with decorative flowers, filling them with a mixture of 7-Up and maraschino cherry juice for toasting each New Year as it arrived. I'd hate for her to spend her last New Year's Eve alone.

I smile at the bright pink slippers at the foot of her bed, remembering the cheap paintings of bouquets and landscapes she used to buy at the Woolworth's five-and-dime. She'd hang them on the walls of our home and then decide they weren't colorful enough. Over time, splashes of bright purple and pink—her favorite colors—appeared in these pictures, odd blossoms suddenly dotting subtly green trees, or popping up among pastel flowers in a vase. Flourishes of uncharacteristic boldness.

Just before midnight, two nurses' aides appear by the bed on a mission to change her diaper, rousing her gently. As they pull down the bed covers and lift her nightgown, Mom moves her hands to cover herself, uncomfortable with the exposure. When they roll her toward me, a look of terror overtakes her face as she cries out and reaches for the bedrail. Eyes wide, staring blankly in my direction, she sustains a chorus of moans that sound to me like a mourner's keening.

～◦∕⌒∕◦～

It's Thanksgiving 2004. We're in my sister Kay's North Carolina home, where our extended family has converged for a traditional Thanksgiving feast. Before dinner, in response to my mother's offer to set the table, I hand her the silverware. Minutes later, I discover her standing by the dining room table, still clutching the utensils, utterly bewildered. My sisters and I have witnessed other signs of Mom's failing memory, but this is the day we know for certain that we are on the long journey with the identity thief known as Alzheimer's.

After the meal, I find Mom in the kitchen by the turkey carcass. She's pulling off scraps of meat and lobbing them across the room at Kay's two dogs. The larger one—whose ear was accidentally clipped during a pre-Thanksgiving trim—is wearing one of those pathetically comic lampshade contraptions that dogs wear to keep them from messing with their wounds.

A piece of turkey lands between the dog's jowl and his unique head ornament, sending him into a frenzy in an effort to dislodge it. For several minutes, we watch as this 100-pound golden retriever lacking peripheral vision careens off walls and knocks into furniture, with an 85-pound chocolate lab barking at his heels, and our mother pelting their backsides with meat and shouting, "Catch!" If we needed a metaphor for the journey upon which we were embarking, we had just been given one.

Over the years, my sisters Kay and Debra and I watched our mother slowly lose ground. She forgot how to tell time, misplaced her car in the parking lot outside the grocery store, fed herself and her eighteen-year-old cat a diet of pickled beets and key lime pie. One Christmas she hid from a twelve-foot-long albino alligator with blue eyes that she believed was stalking her—a chapter in her story that a friend refers to as "ereptile dysfunction."

Feeling myopic and disoriented at each step, we nonetheless threw ourselves into making the best decisions we could about our mother's care, watching rather helplessly as her world shrank from the two-story home in which my sisters and I grew up, to half a duplex in a retirement community, to a small room in an assisted-living facility, to a bed in a nursing home specializing in dementia care.

On her February birthday in 2010, Mom fell and broke her cheek-bone on the edge of a table. For weeks her face looked battered, her eyes swollen almost shut. She began sleeping more hours than she stayed awake, often dozing in a chair through our visits.

In July Mom told my sisters and me she was ready to die. Able to articulate little else, she spoke this wish several times with clarity, and we got her admitted to hospice care at her nursing home. She began having regular conversations with a long-dead cousin and told us it was time to gather the family.

⁂

Flanked by her three daughters, Mom shuffles slowly down a dark hallway into her facility's community room, where the rest of her family and her favorite home-cooked ham-and-potatoes meal are waiting. The room is flooded with bright sunlight from a bank of windows on the far wall, and her grandchildren and sons-in-law appear at first blinking glance as haloed silhouettes. Kay's husband reaches out his arms to Mom and says, "We've been waiting for you."

She cries out and falls back, as her daughters quickly move in to catch her. Then our mother stands up straight and charges into that room with more energy than we have observed in months. Kay, Debra, and I share the conviction that Mom believed that she was being welcomed into heaven and couldn't get there fast enough.

The months that followed were agonizing, as we struggled to honor her wish to die, in an institution that was committed to keeping residents alive as long as possible—several of them in a near-vegetative state. We saw our mother's grim future in their vacant stares.

At lunch one day, I observed three caregivers hovering around a resident. One was trying to shove a spoonful of mashed potatoes into her mouth, while another held her jaw open and a third massaged her shoulders in an effort to get her to relax and stop clenching. Perhaps her family members expected this treatment for their loved one, but Kay, Debra, and I were united in our feeling that this policy of aggressive coaxing and manipulation was inhumane.

Kay and I requested a meeting with the facility's new director. We were hoping for a compassionate conversation in which we were allies together in our concern for what was best for our mother. We walked into a room where half a dozen facility and hospice personnel were waiting.

The director launched the conversation with his views on Dr. Kevorkian, apparently finding the renowned "suicide doctor" relevant to our situation. He moved on to tell us about his own service as a medic in Vietnam, where he wore holsters of morphine, and young soldiers "maimed and burned beyond recognition," pleaded with him to end their suffering permanently. He would not.

And neither would he kill our mother, the director informed us. The facility would continue to make her eat, until she reached the predictable end of many people with end-stage Alzheimer's. One day, he explained, our mother would forget how to swallow, aspirate on her food, and die of pneumonia. He seemed not to understand that this was precisely the horror we were there hoping to prevent.

The director then handed us a letter written in legalese. The opening line described our simple request that our mother not be force-fed as "your cease and desist order." He ended the conversation by challenging us to sue him.

To our great relief and gratitude, the wonderful Solace hospice center in Asheville, North Carolina, where I live, admitted Mom for a transitional stay while we figured out our next step. Over a period of ten weeks there, she lost her ability to walk and to swallow solid food, became totally incontinent, and declined in her already severely compromised speech and comprehension.

But still, always eager to please, she opened her mouth reflexively like a baby bird whenever anything was put near her mouth. She attempted to eat a paper napkin as predictably as she ate food. We knew that she could exist in this state—and worse—for a very long time. And that putting her in another nursing home would make that likely.

⸎

Kay, Debra, and I are sharing lunch at my favorite Mexican restaurant, not far from the small farm on the edge of Asheville where I live with friends. We know that we have to move Mom. We're wondering if we need to do another round of visiting nursing homes, troubled that the ones we've already seen have found our questions uncomfortable and have expressed their unwavering commitment to feeding their residents pureed food, Ensure, or whatever it takes to keep them alive. While we recognize that this is compassionate care in many circumstances, we are together in our belief that this is it is not what our mother wants.

There's more silence than talk as we nibble on our blue-corn nachos and begin to despair over our options. I break the tension with a quiet declaration: "What I really want is for the three of us to move into the farmhouse and care for Mom to the end."

A brief pause while this sinks in. Then, with tears streaming down her face, Debra says, "I'm in." And Kay agrees that this is the best course.

I had proposed caring for Mom at home the previous summer, after our meeting at her facility went so badly. But though our parents had secured generous insurance to cover long-term care in a facility, they had declined the in-home care benefit—part of their longstanding desire not to be a burden on their daughters. And my sisters and I were not at all convinced that we had the collective physical, emotional, and spiritual stamina necessary for the task. But what pushed us to clarity was the realization that bringing Mom home was the only way to avoid prolonging her suffering and save her from a slow, languishing, and debilitating dying.

My sisters, bless them, put their regular lives on hold and moved to the farm at the end of January 2011. Nothing really prepared us to care for our mother in her final days. Except, of course, thousands of years of human history. Only those of us with modern sensibilities and resources have the capacity to isolate ourselves from the intimacies, both harsh and tender, of dying.

‿♔‿

Mom has been at the farm for four days, settled in a hospital bed by a picture window with a sweeping view of our extensive, though dormant for the winter, garden. Flowers from caring friends are arranged along the sill. We are sustained by a generous community of loved ones near and far, who have showered us with messages and massages and meals. Plus plenty of chocolate.

I call my nephew, the new father whose daughter was born just a week ago. I ask him how it's going. "We're pretty exhausted," he says. "Changing a lot of diapers. Up every few hours. Checking regularly to make sure she's still breathing."

That describes our life in the farmhouse exactly. As I survey the stacks of diapers, the lotions and cleansers, the swabs and wipes and sippy cups that have suddenly overtaken my home, I think, "Dying sure is a lot like being born."

My sisters and I have settled into a routine, dragging out old jigsaw puzzles and playing Bananagrams to pass the time, watching favorite DVDs, eating hot fudge sundaes every evening in honor of our upbringing in Hershey, Pennsylvania. When the visiting hospice nurse tells us that meat is now too difficult for Mom to digest, we three mostly vegetarians have to decide what to do with a pound of ground beef. Kay has the brilliant idea of making "hobo stew"—a staple from our childhood camping days that involves wrapping sliced potatoes, carrots, and onions in foil with ground beef—and cooking it in the fireplace. Good with lots of ketchup.

The rest of the world seems to slip away as Mom's needs fill our days. One week into it, Debra says to me at the end of a particularly difficult day for Mom's bowels (and therefore for us as well), "I think we're the only two people in the country who don't know who won the Super Bowl." We're beginning to wonder how long we can keep at this.

I have a calendar marked with bold stripes, a different color for each of my sisters and me, and for a friend who has agreed to spell us in a month. We've got two months mapped out, with at least two of us covering Mom's needs at all times. But we already know it won't be much longer.

On the eve of my mother's passing, Kay, Debra, and I gather around her bed, read a psalm and sing her a lullaby, as we have every evening since bringing her to the farm. Before tucking her in, we turn on the porch light beyond the window to soften the darkness, its glow falling on the two items that hang above her bed: her favorite painting of Jesus tenderly holding a lamb and her Do Not Resuscitate order.

It's my turn to take the night shift. I feel like a midwife, timing my mother's breaths by my watch as expectant parents would time contractions, increasing the dosage and frequency of morphine through that long night drenched in moonlight. "Don't worry," the hospice nurse had told us, counting the syringes she had brought, "there's not enough here to kill her"—apparently missing the irony. Or maybe wanting to reassure us.

My mother took her last breath a little before eleven o'clock in the morning on February 13, 2011. I choose to believe that, a free soul unencumbered by her failing body and bewildered mind, she flew with all the joy and determination we had witnessed a few months earlier into heaven and the outstretched arms of One saying tenderly, "We've been waiting for you."

⋯⋯

As I help the hospice nurse gently bathe her body, I think back to the day two weeks before when Kay and Debra and I brought Mom to the farm. She had never been there before, and she hadn't recognized her daughters in almost two years. But when her head hit the pillow of the hospital bed, she smiled at us and said, "I'm home."

Three days later, she stopped eating and drinking. She began responding "no" and "not really" when we offered her food and drink, and then consistently turned her head away. Kay, Debra, and I acknowledged that we had given Mom a gift by bringing her to the farm, and she had given one back to us. She saved us the anguish of deciding for her.

This was both what we had hoped for and a cause of some concern. My sisters and I had discovered through our long process of advocacy on behalf of our mother that we are rare among families. The norm, it seems, is that at least one family member—often more—needs to be convinced to let go of a loved one.

But back when our mother was totally lucid—and watching a relative suffer the indignities of Alzheimer's for almost a decade—she informed us on several occasions that she did not want to live with severe dementia. She signed advance directives, hoping to ensure that her life would not be prolonged under such a circumstance.

Our one desire was to honor her wish. We were convinced that, if alongside the statements declining CPR, a ventilator, and a feeding tube, she could have signed her name under, "If I cannot feed myself, please don't feed me," she would have. But those words do not yet exist on advance directives.

My sisters and I knew when we brought Mom home that we were stepping into murky moral terrain, and we wrestled mightily to find solid ground. In an effort to make as informed and compassionate a decision as possible, we consulted an array of chaplains, ethicists, and hospice personnel.

One who was sympathetic to our plight pointed out the irony that our honesty had drawn attention to ourselves. She mentioned her legal obligation to report us to Adult Protective Services if we refused home hospice care, which would be interpreted as an indication that we were intending not to feed our mother. Her concern was unwarranted; my sisters and I never considered refusing the services of hospice personnel, whose competence and compassion were invaluable to us.

I remembered a friend in chaplaincy training who had told me about a European doctor visiting the nursing home where she was serving. Surveying the state of the residents, he had asked, "Don't you let people die in this country?" Indeed.

We will not much longer be able to afford, either morally or financially, the prolonged sustenance of our elders who have no discernible quality of life. We simply will not be able to pay the billions required for institutional care for the millions of my baby-boomer generation who will lose our minds.

At its best, our current morality around mortality is an indictment of a culture that refuses to accept death and limits. At its worst, it's a profit-making venture for some that will bankrupt the rest of us. We can only hope that financial crisis and common sense will eventually push and then rearrange our end-of-life ethical landscape. But we're not there yet.

For a brief moment, my sisters and I considered whether we needed to make our mother eat for a while. We knew it would appear suspicious to have her die so soon after we had brought her home. I'm grateful that we named the absurdity of that thought and chose to honor and celebrate our mother's clarity amid the fog of her dementia. Still, we felt enough concern that we videotaped her refusing food. To cover ourselves.

Some of the people we encountered would say that we killed our mother. But my sisters and I know that we did not. She was gone long before we took over her care. And so we are left with a feeling a friend of mine calls "grelief"—that poignant mix of grief and relief.

The day Mom died—weeks before spring was officially scheduled to arrive—fifteen tiny, delicate, teardrop-shaped white flowers appeared by the pond beyond the picture window. One for each day of our vigil with our mother at the farm. When I glimpsed their beauty and boldness, I thought again: "Dying sure is a lot like being born."

The mortuary men pull up in their black SUV, one almost seven feet tall and the other short and wearing cowboy boots, a Blue Tooth clamped on his ear. Kay had managed to locate in the back of a closet at her home the purple dress our mother wore at my nephew's wedding in the summer of 2003—the last time she wore a dress. The men who have come for her body ask about her stockings and heels. These had not occurred to us.

Mom hated wearing these in life, and we can see no earthly (or heavenly) reason why she should wear them in a closed casket for death. "Here, take these," Kay insists, handing over the bright pink bedroom slippers to the stunned mortuary men. We don't know for sure, but I like to believe that under the huge spray of pink and purple lilies, carnations, and irises on her casket, Mom was wearing her purple dress and those bright pink slippers.

At the funeral, Kay, Debra, and I share tears and reach for one another when a soloist sings the lullaby with which we serenaded our mother on hushed and tender nights. We are bone-weary but grateful beyond words for the blessing of accompanying her in her final days—a holy time that deepened the bond that has held us since birth and gave us memories to cherish forever.

In a gently eloquent eulogy, the pastor reflects that sometimes we can look at the horizon and see a sky filled with hues of pink and purple. Sunrise or sunset? The end of the day is like its beginning. The end of a life as well.

4

Why I Build Coffins

Tom Karlin

THIS ANTHOLOGY IS A chance for me to share with fellow travelers my journey to discover the works of mercy. I am a retired self-employed woodworker. In the last thirty-five to forty years I have built many coffins and cremains urns for individuals belonging to communities such as the Tacoma Catholic Worker and L'Arche Tahoma Hope.[1] I've also built many coffins and urns for family, friends, and others seeking alternatives to the products the funeral service industry provides. My primary motive for building them is that it allows me to share more intimately someone's grief in the loss of a loved one.

There are a number of other reasons I have been drawn toward handcrafting items for burials. I wanted to help reduce the cost of funerals, especially for people who struggle financially. It provides a simple and humble vessel for holding the body. It is a way family members and friends can be more involved, by helping me build the coffin or urn. It also raises awareness about our overdependence on death care for profit.

I see the works of mercy as a call to discipleship. We can respond to this call by walking closely with each other through good times as well as illness, death, and burial. "Bear one another's burdens, and in this way you will fulfill the law of Christ" (Gal 6:2).

---

1. L'Arche is an international organization of Christian communities in which people of different physical and developmental abilities live and work together to provide homes and workplaces for people with developmental disabilities.

Growing up as Catholic kids, we had to memorize the Seven Corporal Works of Mercy: to feed the hungry, to give drink to the thirsty, to clothe the naked, to harbor the harborless, to visit the sick, to ransom the captive, and to bury the dead. We also had to memorize the Seven Spiritual Works of Mercy: to instruct the ignorant, to counsel the doubtful, to console the sorrowful, to reprove or correct the sinner, to forgive injuries, to bear wrongs patiently, and to pray for the living and the dead.

Now, as an adult Catholic or Christian, I prefer to think of the Works of Mercy as, rather, Works of Compassion. It seems to me that mercy is more about a relationship with others we might have power over, whereas compassion is more about a relationship of shared suffering. *Cum passio*, means to suffer with. The important thing, whether we call it mercy or compassion, is to recognize and walk with Christ daily under the many disguises through which he is in our midst, as Catholic Worker co-founder Dorothy Day would say.

When I reflect on the much neglected work of mercy to bury the dead, it strikes me that we, as church, as society, have had a great deal of practice neglecting the other works before death, so that neglecting burial of the dead comes only as a natural consequence. It seems to me that if I can recognize Christ under many disguises in the hungry, homeless, the sick, the imprisoned, etc., I will also be able to recognize him in those who have died and respond as he would have us respond (Matt 25:31–46).

Recently, I read an article in the *National Catholic Reporter* that addresses one looming aspect of the neglect of this work of mercy, the rising number of unclaimed bodies across the country. According to the article,[2] Los Angeles County buried more than 1,600 unclaimed people last December. In 2011, Oregon saw a 30 percent increase in unclaimed bodies cremated through its Indigent Burial Fund.

The way we neglect this work of mercy is in sharp contrast to my early roots. When my great-grandparents came from Russia in the 1880s to settle in Kansas, they came as part of a community. In rural Kansas of that day, the death care industry was virtually nonexistent. The farm village community did not have the ability or the need to hire people to accompany their sick and dying or to prepare the bodies of their dead for burial. Farm villagers built the coffins, dug the graves in the small parish cemetery, and buried their dead as a community. No need for a funeral

---

2. Brian Rowe, "Louisiana cemetery to take in unclaimed bodies," *National Catholic Reporter* (April 28, 2012); online: ncronline.org/news/faith-parish/louisiana-cemetery-take-unclaimed-bodies.

directing staff, hearse, embalming, or a concrete vault for the coffin to be placed in. Even the cemeteries were maintained by the community members, with no one expecting payment.

Fast forward: today we have child care for profit, elder care for profit, prisons for profit, death care for profit, etc. We as Church have, perhaps unwittingly, been more influenced by our capitalism than by the Gospel and have gone along, outsourcing even our works of mercy.

Having said that, I do realize that not all for-profit institutions are only in it for money. My younger brother, a quadriplegic, had to go to a skilled care home because family and friends could no longer provide the total around-the-clock care he needed. We found a nursing home in Kansas that gave extraordinary care for less than half the cost of care of the same magnitude here in Washington State, and the care and cleanliness of the facility were exceptional. The same, I know, is true for childcare in many cases. My own children have had to make use of childcare, having needs greater than they and our grandparenting can provide, so good childcare outside the home becomes crucial and can be found. Still I think it is important to outsource care of our vulnerable as infrequently as possible, not only because of financial cost, but even more, for the benefits of cultivating our relationships with our loved ones, sharing more intimately joys and sorrows and the responsibilities and blessings of living and dying together.

Over fifty years ago I experienced two beautiful, simple, and low-cost funerals where no death care for profit organizations were involved. As a young man in the Navy in the 1950s, I was touched deeply by the burial at sea of one of our ship's crew members. The body of our fellow sailor was simply wrapped in a shroud along with weights and placed on a bier (a stretcher-like stand) near the edge of the ship's flight deck. The ship's crew not on duty (over two thousand, or two-thirds of the total crew), were in formation on the flight deck for the service. Near the end of the service, while the ship's chaplain prayed over the body, two sailors gently lifted the bier from the head end and the body was released into the sea.

This burial at sea revealed to me that day, and I'm quite sure revealed to most of the sailors present, several important things. One was the message of my own mortality delivered so early in life, when I had barely begun to seek to understand what it means to become a mature and responsible adult and human being. Another was the beauty of the simple ritual, with so many men of my age present.

The burial at sea was beautifully simple, in spite of the fact that the delivery system (a huge Navy war ship carrying nuclear weapons) was anything but simple or in itself about works of mercy or compassion. At my age then, I had never thought of what it meant to have a consistent ethic of life. I had been taught by my church and trained by the military that, in effect, the Gospel and the Pentagon had co-equal claim on my allegiance.

A few years later after my discharge from the Navy, I entered a Trappist monastery in Oregon. Not long after becoming a monk in 1960, one of our older monks was dying of cancer. The morning of his death, the monastery's bells rang the call for assembly at our brother's deathbed. All sixty-five monks came together from their places of work and began chanting the psalms and prayers for our dying brother—from the hallway and some from inside the infirmary. We all remained until our brother died an hour and a half later. Some of our monks prepared his body for the funeral Mass and burial to be held two hours later. The body was simply dressed in the monk's habit such as we all wore daily, and placed on a bier and brought to the church from the infirmary. In the front of the church near the altar, the body rested, surrounded by tall candle stands.

Some of our monks had already dug a grave right next to the church inside the monastic enclosure. Immediately after the funeral Mass, we all processed to the burial site following the monks carrying the bier with the body of their brother. At the gravesite, more prayers and psalms were sung. Then the abbot pulled the hood of the habit over the head and face, and with a safety pin, pinned it to the chest. Now the body was ready to be gently lowered into the bottom of the grave. We all took turns placing earth around our brother's body and filling up the grave. To this day, Trappist monks still bury their dead the way they have for centuries. Today we would call it "green burial" and a radical concept in America.

My seven years in the monastery right after the four years in the Navy reawakened in me the call to discipleship, that is, participating in the paschal mystery of Christ. By paschal mystery I mean Christ's journey through his life, death and resurrection. I believe Paul's embracing of this mystery is articulated in his letter to the Philippians when he was in prison in Ephesus. "I want to know Christ and the power of his resurrection and the sharing of his sufferings by becoming like him in his death, if somehow I may attain the resurrection from the dead," (Phil 3:10–11).

The Trappists follow the rule of St. Benedict, from the fourth century CE. His motto for himself and the monks was *ora et labora* (prayer and work). The monk's work was prayer and his prayer was his work—inseparable—*ad majorem Dei gloriam* (for the greater glory of God). St. Benedict wanted monks to treat the tools of the monastery as gently and with such care as if they were the sacred vessels of the altar. The brothers were to be treated likewise, since they are the body of Christ.

We monks were taught that work is not just a means for making a living (much less profit) or an obligation to fulfill a contract, but that it has a deeper dignity. There is a special honor conferred on each human being (and I believe, on all creation), and that is the privilege of cooperating with the Creator's work. Furthermore, we were taught that work is also a joy even when it is difficult and seems burdensome, because through it, we build each other up and share in its fruits. When I build coffins or urns for cremains I try to be aware of this approach to *ora et labora*.

The very first coffin I built was for our two-month-old son who died unexpectedly in 1974. I had a cabinet shop right by our house, being self-employed, so it was easy to build a little coffin. Our awareness of all the negative dimensions of the death care industry was quite limited at the time. For my wife Ida and me, building a coffin together was an organic way for us to share our grief, experience the gift of God's presence, and deepen our relationship for the present and for life's journey together ahead. The planning of our son's burial service and the coming together of family and community also gave us strength, courage, and healing. This helped deepen our faith, spurring a commitment to reach out and help others who were in a similar need.

Several years later a young couple in our parish lost their only child unexpectedly to illness. The little girl was three years old. The parents of the couple came and asked if I would build a coffin for the little girl and if they could all help. Working together in the shop with the grieving family was such a gift to Ida and me that we started offering this opportunity to others who were grieving the loss of a loved one.

In 1978, my father-in-law died of a heart ailment. I built his coffin: a simple wood coffin made of local western cedar. Again, my wife and other family members were involved all the way through the burial rites, however, the funeral home was in charge of embalming, hearse, and burial. It wasn't until I saw the cost of this funeral, even though we had provided the coffin, that I became aware of economic and ecological facets of the death care for profit enterprise.

Since 1978, the cost of a funeral has become so prohibitively expensive that people of meager means can't even afford the coffin. For this reason, I have never charged to build a coffin. A simple coffin made from locally grown wood (cedar, alder, or pine) is usually under one hundred dollars. The cost includes the cushioning material and hardware and oil finish. Building a coffin usually takes about twelve hours. Sometimes people have made a freewill offering of the materials' cost or more as a gift of gratitude.

In 1994 my wife Ida died of cancer at age forty-six. Several of my siblings came to live with us during her six-month illness. A brother and two sisters who are nuns, one of them a hospice worker, took turns staying with us and our four children, ages twelve to twenty-one. The whole journey with my wife, the children, our families and friends, was a living of the paschal mystery together as we understood it in the midst of that passage. We built the coffin, and when Ida died, we were all at her side. We took her body in our van to the funeral home, just the four children and me. On the day of the burial Mass, again, the children and I picked up Ida's body, now in the coffin, took it to the church, and after the service took the coffin in our van to the cemetery for burial. After the burial, a large potluck gathering was held at our farm home.

Again, I'd like to speak of the paschal mystery—the life, death, and resurrection of Jesus—and our participation in this mystery. It's been eighteen years since our family's immersion in the death of Ida. Our family and community have also participated in resurrection through healing, growing closer, and deepening our discipleship. I believe that resurrection and eternal life are in the here and now for us all, just as life and death are. Whenever we replace hatred with love, violence with nonviolence, consumerism with simple living, and perform random acts of kindness, we are practicing resurrection.

A book by Henri Nouwen has been so helpful to me and my family for caregiving and being with our dying friends. This little book is only about one hundred pages and is called *Our Greatest Gift: A Meditation on Dying and Caring.*[3] In the early 1980s, our family had the privilege of having Henri live with us for a month when he needed a break from his very demanding schedule back east. When Ida was dying, he sent the little book which became such an important guide and support for our family through all we had to bear. I have given copies of this book to many family members and friends entering the same walk. Henri's friendship was a gift that has kept enriching us even after his death in 1996.

3. Henri M. J. Nouwen, *Our Greatest Gift: A Meditation on Dying and Caring* (San Francisco: Harper San Francisco, 1994).

In 2000 I was blessed with a companion to continue my life journey. Laura and I got married and joined the Catholic Worker community in Tacoma where our resurrection work took the form of hospitality in the urban core and drawing connections between militarism and poverty. After almost seven years there, we took a leave to be with three of my siblings who were dying of cancer in three different states: Montana, Kansas, and Wisconsin. It was a gift of grace to be with my siblings and their families, walking with them through illness, suffering, dying, and preparing their bodies for burial. For a brother and a sister, I built the urns for the deposition of their ashes. Together with the families, we prepared the burial rituals and buried the urns above the grave of my father and mother in the small parish cemetery in Kansas, miles out of town off a country road in a wheat field.

I have reflected on the work of mercy *to bury the dead* every time I have had the opportunity to build a coffin. Every Holy Week when I hear the readings of Jesus' passion and death, I'm moved by the person of Joseph of Arimathea in all four gospels. "So Joseph took the body and wrapped it in a clean linen cloth and laid it in his own new tomb, which he had hewn in the rock" (Matt 27:59–60a). Think of the privilege we have with Joseph to bury Jesus when we do it for the least of these sisters and brothers in our midst.

Much of what I have been sharing could be described as quite radical, part of the "fringe" green burial movement. But over and over, people have told me how much they desire to have better burial options when their loved one dies, and have felt hopeless and helpless to find any. What is such a hopeful and helpful sign now is that green burial options are moving out of the fringe and into mainstream consciousness. This movement has been advanced by the extraordinary work of many people involved with the Green Burial Council. Since 2005 when the council was established, it has involved environmentalists, scientists, lawyers, religious organizations, representatives of the funeral service industry, and many other diverse and often disparate groups or organizations. By involving all these people of good will, the Green Burial Council has been able to establish death care and deposition standards that give us access to new options, yes, even such as the Trappists have always had!

This movement's development is growing rapidly across the US and in Canada. Please check out the Green Burial Council's website at http://greenburialcouncil.org or contact them at 550-D St. Michaels Drive, Santa Fe, NM 87505; (888) 966–3300. The website will answer almost any question you may have about green burial. Its vision begins: "We want to see eco-friendly end of life rituals become a viable option for honoring the dead, healing the living, and inviting the Divine."

May it be so.

5

Thoughts on Burying My Mother, Brother, and, of course, John[1]

JEFF DIETRICH

WE MADE A BIZARRE-LOOKING funeral procession as we pulled away from the mortuary—no hearse, no limousines, no motorcycle police to clear the traffic; just a battered old pick-up with the coffin lashed to the back, followed in quick succession by a handful of nondescript vehicles. Somehow in the rush we forgot to bring the tarp, so anyone who wished could see we were transporting the coffin that contained the earthly remains of John Slowikowski.

About halfway up the winding mountain road, we lost sight of the pick-up truck. Backtracking, we found it in a convenience store parking lot, everyone politely ignoring the coffin while John's brothers dashed into the store to purchase a couple cases of beer.

Death is the essential human experience but within American culture there is a strenuous reluctance even at funerals to admit to what theologian William Stringfellow called the Power of death.[2] This is part

1. Versions of this article have appeared as "Blessed Are Those Who Mourn," *Catholic Agitator* 24/2 (1993) 3, 6; and as "Thoughts on Burying My Mother, Brother and, of course, John," *National Catholic Reporter*, October 22, 1993, 20, and are reprinted here with permission.

2. William Stringfellow, "Christ and the Powers of Death," in *William Stringfellow in Anglo-American Perspective*, edited by Anthony Dancer (Burlington, VT: Ashgate, 2005), 57–65.

and parcel of a deeper pathology. Our desire to distance ourselves from the experience of death reflects an abiding faith in the cultural delusions of progress and utopia. The only life we affirm is that narrow range of existence that is lived most powerfully in the marketplace and the laboratory. The denial of death is essential to the maintenance of our most important cultural values. Because we are distanced from any authentic form of life, we thus find ourselves distanced from death.

If we for one minute stopped believing in the possibility of salvation through higher education, professionalism, financial investment and career development, the entire social system might collapse. It is the consciousness of our own death that separates the human species from all other forms of life. Yet, the effort that is made to remove and sanitize death is possibly the hallmark of our culture.

As we bounced along the slush-clogged road bearing John's body deeper into the darkening winter forest I reflected that so much of my life at the Catholic Worker has been a form of mourning. Our work of feeding and serving the poor brings us into unavoidable contact with the forces of death. Our culture, says scripture scholar Walter Brueggemann, is committed to numbness about death. "The task of prophetic imagination is to cut through the numbness, to penetrate the self-deception so that the God of endings is confessed as Lord."[3]

This process of numbness and self-deception finds its roots in the arts of the undertaker. The distancing and professionalization of that which should be intimate and personal is the first step in our denial of death. In my own case, I have always regretted never having said good-bye to my brother. But after his suicide in 1973, I was unable to bring myself face-to-face with the pain and guilt of his death. I just wanted him in the ground, thinking his burial would somehow end my pain. Of course the funeral industry was most obliging in helping me avoid any contact with the experience of my brother's death.

It is impossible to grieve without the object of our grief, and it is precisely this experience that the contemporary funeral industry robs us of. I felt like a sleep-walker, going through the motions. It would take many years before I could wake up and experience my experience of Joe's death.

In some cultures, and in our own not too distant past, when community and tradition still existed, people took care of their dead. They had neither the luxury nor the desire to pay another to do it. Death and

3. Walter Brueggemann, *The Prophetic Imagination*, 2nd ed. (Minneapolis: Fortress, 2001), 45.

grieving took place at home, not at a mortuary. Like most simpler arrangements, it was also a healthier and more integrated experience. But for us, those simpler arrangements are long gone and we no longer know how to deal with death or even how to behave in its presence.

We learned this dramatic lesson in our own community when little Maria died. She had lived with us for two years, capturing everyone's heart, before finally succumbing to cancer at age five.

Due to our community's poverty and perverseness, we decided to resist convention and do the funeral ourselves. A carpenter friend built her a coffin, and my sister bought Maria's laying-out dress. Because Maria had just missed making her first communion, her mother wanted a white communion dress. But Maria's cancer-ravaged body was so tiny, she had to wear a baptismal gown.

We drove our old Chevy van to the mortuary and picked up little Maria. We placed her tiny homemade coffin on our coffee table, in the midst of a beautiful arrangement of flowers. But now we had a dead body in the house, and we were not sure what to do next.

Twenty Latina women from the neighborhood, friends of Maria and her mother, arrived to vigil with us. They prayed their rosaries, chanted litanies and sang about a hundred songs. By their very presence, these women created a sense of intimacy and reverence. They were familiar with death and unafraid. In the dining room we served food and refreshments, and while some ate, others kept quiet vigil.

The next morning we put Maria in the van and drove her to the church where we were greeted by a score of her little friends from school who escorted her down the aisle to the altar. After the service, we drove her out to the cemetery for the burial.

I am certain it was the experience with little Maria's death that gave me the courage, four months later when my mother died, to suggest that we have a home wake for her. But I might as well have been demanding that we have a nude funeral, for all the enthusiasm my suggestion evoked.

It is difficult, for any of us, confronted with the death of a loved one, to attempt something out of the ordinary. Nevertheless, I gained an amazing insight into the power of community from my mother's death. My mother was well-liked in her parish and had many friends. So, as soon as word went out that she had died, people began arriving with casseroles, cakes and other culinary expressions of their concern. At first, I thought this was rather intrusive, but gradually I realized that as each new person arrived, wanting all the details of what had happened, the pain of mother's death would diminish a tiny bit each time it was shared.

Soon the house was filed with friends and relatives. It seemed like a grand party as people ate and drank and told their favorite stories about my mother. It made me wish all the more we had the courage to break convention and have my mother at home.

Back to John. It was late morning when Catherine got the phone call from her sister, Eileen, "John is dead. You have to come now." We drove through the night, reaching Oregon before dawn the next day.

John had died at age twenty-nine, violently and tragically at the hands of another while on vacation in Mexico. The pain of his death was compounded by a lack of information. Due to the barriers of language and culture, there seemed to be no adequate answers to the questions of why, how, and who is responsible? In the meantime, his body was shipped back by air-freight in just two days. I suggested that whatever else they did, the family should consider bringing John back home to the house where he had grown up, where they had lived together.

I found that it was a simple matter in Oregon to have a burial on your own property. I suggested they would like to bury him at Greensprings, the family cabin in the mountains and a place that John particularly loved. The response was an enthusiastic one, especially from John's brothers, who completed part of the project that night before official permission had been secured. They gathered some friends, took shovels, picks, lanterns and a bottle of Jack Daniels. They dug through the night pulling out rocks and stones the size of bowling balls. They dug it deep—it must have been well over seven feet. As they dug, they talked about John, cried and drank some Jack Daniels. It was almost dawn when they finished. They had worked off some of their grief, their anger, and their guilt in this last gift they would ever give their brother.

Catherine and her sister Eileen got up in the morning to prepare for the wake. First they cleared out the back bedroom and cleaned it. They brought in three potted pine trees, some pictures of John and set up his prized arrowhead collection. John's body arrived from the funeral home at four o'clock, and the family gathered in the back room to greet him. In the living room, friends and neighbors had already come over with food. There was plenty of wine.

People were invited to come back and see John. At first, it was a little formal, but soon there was a large group in the room and they started to talk to John and to each other—remembering a party, a camping trip, a high school experience.

In the beginning they touched him only very tentatively—"Oh, you are so cold, John." But quickly it was more intimate. "Oh, John, this is the last time I will ever kiss you," said his girlfriend, Mary, as she gently pressed her lips against his. The wake went on into the night, people eating and drinking, laughing and crying, and saying good-bye to John.

John stayed with us through the night, and in the morning the community of mourners gathered again at the house for a funeral service. A few prayers were said and many stories were told.

It was almost dark by the time we reached the gravesite. The coffin was heavy and the husky boys carrying it slipped a few times before they reached the place where lodge pole saplings straddled the open grave, making a perch for the coffin.

About thirty people gathered in the waning winter light and told more stories, opened the coffin for a final good-bye, stuffed in a few candy bars and the empty bottle of Jack Daniels. Then with a final good-bye we lowered him into the ground. Paul passed out the shovels and everyone took a turn filling in the grave. "Save the stones until last," he said. "They can go on top so that the earth can settle more evenly."

As the moon came up over the Eastern Siskiyou Mountains, we gathered around the grave holding hands for a final prayer.

I believe in the resurrection and life everlasting. But I must confess that I do not know very much about resurrection. However, I am convinced that most Christians put far too much emphasis on resurrection and the afterlife, and far too little upon the crucifixion and death. I am reminded that while the disciples were holed up in fear and denial, it was the women who took spices and ointments to anoint Jesus. And because of their willingness to touch the body of the dead, they were the first to see the resurrection. I am convinced that eternal life will be ours only if we have the courage to embrace the experience of death.

6

Caretaking the Gift
A Journey of Hospice

ELAINE ENNS AND CHED MYERS

*In the spiritual realm, something
is set in motion by every true act of faith.*
—LADON SHEATS

ON GOOD FRIDAY 2002, while in Lubbock, Texas, caretaking his ninety-three
year-old father, our dear friend Homer Ladon Sheats discovered that he had
become strangely jaundiced. A week later, after exploratory surgery, he was
diagnosed with terminal pancreatic cancer. We were in Greensboro, North
Carolina, helping to run the first Word and World School,[1] and the news
hit our hearts like a sledgehammer. We immediately left to join Tensie Her-
nandez and Dennis Apel of the Guadalupe Catholic Worker and several of
Ladon's family members and friends at his bedside in a Lubbock hospital.

It was an intense and difficult week. We were all in shock. The last
time any of us had seen Ladon he had been in good health; now he looked
awful. We didn't know whether he'd make it out of the hospital alive, and
our late-night conversation centered on where we could bury him—and
how to transport his body (illegally) across state lines.

1. Online: www.wordandworld.org

Buoyed by prayer and our round-the-clock presence, Ladon rebounded. He decided not to try any further medical intervention, and we set about discerning how and where to take him for hospice. We were ill-prepared, but not half-hearted; this man was so important to us that we would do whatever it took to give him a good space to finish his journey.

Some years before, Tensie had told Ladon that she wished to care for him when he was infirm. Now the moment had arrived, in a way none of us could have imagined. She reiterated her offer, and without a clue how this would actually happen, Dennis added, "we can build a room in our garage. Our home is yours." Without hesitation Ladon accepted. Now we had to figure out how to get him to California.

Ladon was far too weak to endure a drive across four states. As we were mulling over this conundrum, his brother Morris offered to make a couple of phone calls, "to see about a plane." We shrugged, unaware of the fact that Morris—at that time the pastor of a wealthy Dallas mega-church—actually had *parishioners* with private jets. A few hours later, Morris reported that a Lear Jet had been arranged to fly Ladon and Tensie (as his attendant) from the local private airport to San Luis Obispo, CA.

We looked at each other with incredulity, gratitude, and no small measure of bemusement. It was beyond ironic: the man who thirty-five years previously had walked away from the world of high rolling executive jet-setting in order to commit his life to the poor and to peacemaking would now take one last flight. The next morning we wheeled Ladon out of the hospital onto the tarmac and into the plane, singing "Swing Low, Sweet Chariot."

They arrived hours later in Santa Maria, the central California home of Tensie and Dennis and their two children, Rozella and Thomas. There Ladon—and all of us who helped care for him—began a four-month journey of hospice that was in equal parts taxing and transforming. During this time, ten-month old Thomas Ladon took his first steps and said his first words—and Homer Ladon his last. Dennis and Tensie opened their lives in the deepest possible sense, and a crazy quilt of community arose to the task. It was an act of true faith, and what it set in motion we are still trying to fathom.

୧୨

Find out which way God is moving, and move with it.

—Pastor Homer Sheats (Ladon's father)

Ladon Sheats was born in 1934 in Brownfield, Texas, the middle of three sons. His father, Homer, was an Assemblies of God preacher who pulled cotton by day and built churches by night among the hardscrabble towns of west Texas. His mother, with whom he was exceptionally close, was equally hard working and faithful. Church was their whole life, and Ladon would occasionally spin stories about growing up that were both poignant and hilarious.

After completing a stint in the Air Force and a business degree from Texas Tech, Ladon became a top executive for IBM in the 1960s. In this era of the first great computer technology boom, Ladon came to live large: keeping offices and homes on both coasts, eating at the best restaurants and vacationing all over the world. But he was spiritually uneasy, and thirsted for the faith of his childhood to come alive again, and for the gospel to mean more than it did to most American Christians.

It was a 1967 meeting with Baptist activist-theologian Clarence Jordan that disrupted Ladon's upward mobility and led to a dramatic about-face. Ladon was radically inspired and challenged by Clarence's experiments with interracial farming communities among the poor of south Georgia and his exposition of the Way of Jesus in the gospels. After an agonizing year of discernment, Ladon divested himself of his wealth and went to live at Koinonia Partners in Americus Georgia.[2] Tragically Clarence died just a few months later. But from that time on, Ladon became a living witness to (and interpreter of) Clarence's vision of radical discipleship to many of us around the country.

Ladon expressed his gospel faith in three notable ways:

1. He joined prayer and protest in public witness for peace and an end to the arms race. His resistance to militarism at places such as the Pentagon and military air shows earned him many long stints in jail. A leader for five years at Koinonia, Ladon felt increasingly convicted about the evil of the continuing war in Vietnam, and wished to express more active resistance to it. In 1974 he joined the Jonah

---

2. For a good introduction to Jordan's writings see Hollyday, Joyce ed. *Clarence Jordan: Essential Writings.* Modern Spiritual Masters Series (Maryknoll, NY: Orbis Books, 2009). Online: www.koinoniapartners.org/clarence/index.html

House peace community in Baltimore,[3] where he stayed until 1979, and where he is still dearly loved. After this he initiated a series of prayer pilgrimages at nuclear weapons plants such as Rocky Flats in Colorado and Pantex in Texas. The prison time that resulted from his many acts of nonviolent civil disobedience was hard because of his consistent refusal to cooperate with an oppressive system. Yet his long periods in solitary confinement in some ways also deepened his contemplative spirit. In the 1990s Ladon traveled to Japan and Iraq as a grassroots ambassador for peace and to visit victims of US war-making.

2. A related commitment was service to the poor. Ladon was a fierce critic of first world consumer affluence, while making himself available to hurting and marginalized persons wherever he encountered them. This took him from New York's Lower East Side to rural Georgia to Skid Row in Los Angeles. For the last twenty years of his life, Ladon lived out of a backpack, itinerating around the country between various communities and individuals to offer a hand in their work. He served for long stretches with the L.A. Catholic Worker community.[4] There and elsewhere he became deeply involved in hospice work, for friends (including Kieran Prather[5]) and family as well as homeless persons.

3. Ladon was a man of deep prayer, who desired intensely to know God ever more intimately. He spent many months in solitude, not only involuntarily in prison, but also voluntarily at a Benedictine monastery in Colorado.[6] Ladon was profoundly nurtured by Creation; an avid hiker, he was happiest at an old hermitage cabin at the foot of his beloved Mt. Sopris in Colorado. Yet he was able to appreciate beauty wherever it could be found, from inner city streets to wilderness peaks.

In these and other ways Ladon sought to embody the Way of Jesus that comforts the afflicted and afflicts the comfortable. His discipleship was exemplary in its compassion, stubborn in its spiritual questing, and rich in its generous friendship.

3. Online: www.jonahhouse.org

4. Online: lacatholicworker.org

5. See contributions by and about Kieran in chapters 7–9.

6. Online: www.snowmass.org

Ched first met Ladon at a weekend retreat in 1976, a moment Ched now sees as his "second call to discipleship." At age twenty-one, Ched hitchhiked across the country to Baltimore to join Ladon at Jonah House. In an extraordinary act of hospitality, Ladon offered Ched space in his small room, sacrificing the only refuge he had as an introvert for the sake of a young seeker. From that time on, Ladon became a faithful friend to Ched, as he was for a remarkably wide and diverse circle of us across the US. Elaine met him in 1997, and Ladon made a particular impact on her close-knit Mennonite family when he came up to Saskatchewan for our 1999 wedding.

Ladon was a complex person, a sometimes inscrutable contradiction of intimacy and individualism, mobility and rootedness, initiative and quiet non-directiveness, fierce conviction and humble receptivity. He was the best listener many of us have ever known, with an extraordinary capacity to elicit our individual struggles and dreams, to help us discern, and to stay in touch despite distances. It is fair to say that no one who received Ladon's full attention, and who heard his remarkable story, was not deeply moved and changed.

We won't know if something is true or not unless we try it. I know now that Jesus' invitation to "Seek first the Kingdom, and all else will be provided for you"[7] is true, more reliable than any of the rinky-dink rafts we've lashed together along this river of life.

—LADON SHEATS

Once, when asked if he believed in infant baptism, Mark Twain famously retorted, "Believe it?! Hell, I've *seen* it!" We have come to feel the same way about the divine economy of gift and grace, and though Ched has spoken and written widely on the topic,[8] this hospice journey was perhaps our most concrete experience of that most powerfully alternative reality.

Ladon had no assets, no pension plan, and no health insurance, having bet his life on Jesus' promise that "whosever would release themselves from family, possession, and home would receive them back a hundredfold" (Mark 10:29).[9] His "investments" were exclusively in relationships,

---

7. Matt 6:33

8. See Ched Myers, *The Biblical Vision of Sabbath Economics* (Washington, DC: Tell the Word Press, 2001). Online: www.chedmyers.org/catalog/sabbath-economics

9. Translation by Ched Myers.

in witness, and in service. And it was precisely the amazing web of friendship and care he wove throughout his life that became his "social security." Never have we witnessed such a spontaneous and sustained outpouring of mutual aid, such unquestioned devotion to a friend, such determination to return kindnesses received, than during that hospice effort in central California.

The Guadalupe and Los Angeles Catholic Worker communities and our Bartimaeus Cooperative Ministries (BCM)[10] cobbled together the basic personnel, logistical, financial, and moral resources, then relied heavily on the solidarity of people around the country. Countless individuals and families from Ladon's extraordinary network of friends offered whatever was needed, from prayers and visits to bodywork and cooking, and just enough financial support to cover the costs of this hospice "ad-hocracy."

Gifts flowed in from the Four Directions: hot meals and fresh produce from Santa Barbara, hundreds of origami cranes from Monterey, a sheepskin from the Sierras, flowers, pictures, a walking stick, and dozens of other expressions of love and concern. Each evening for four months a different group sat around the dinner table—never fewer than a half dozen and sometimes three times that many—and joined in community-building times of laughter and storytelling. Many of us finally got to know persons we had always heard of from Ladon, and we formed a special bond with Ladon's brothers, niece and other family members. It was as if Ladon, in this last chapter, was orchestrating a convergence of his widely scattered circles. Here was a parable of death and resurrection: as Ladon's body atrophied, the body of those in communion with him over the years expanded.

In the first six weeks after Ladon arrived, a volunteer crew (some of whom even knew something about building!) converged on Santa Maria to transform a dilapidated garage into a beautiful hospice room. We commuted up from Los Angeles for at least half of every week, and along with visitors and helpers, lodged at Beatitude House of hospitality ten miles west in Guadalupe. When the house was full, we put folk in an old Winnebago loaned by friends and parked in the backyard of the Santa Maria house. Our job was cooking, cleaning, and helping to keep the ongoing activist and hospitality work of the Guadalupe Catholic Worker[11] going. Over four months, more than one hundred people came

---

10. Online: www.bcm-net.org

11. Online: www.catholicworker.org/communities/commlistall.cfm#CA

to join our circle, some for a day or two, some for weeks. BCM developed a website to keep folks abreast, and two phones were steadily in use. Daily prayer circles sustained us, with sage and song drifting through petitions, scripture and silence.

For the first two months Ladon was strong enough to receive most visitors, and occasionally got out for a walk or drive. We celebrated his sixty-eighth birthday in late June with two big parties, beautiful times of commemoration and thanksgiving. After that he declined slowly but steadily, and we had to start limiting visits. Throughout Ladon received loving nursing care—particularly from Tensie—and experienced relatively little pain.

Though the process was exhausting, we were always mindful that we were in the midst of a miracle of grace, of "just enough for the day," as the Lord's Prayer puts it. Indeed, every time we had a need, someone showed up who had the right skills, whether fixing plumbing, laying tile—or building a coffin.

◦⌾◦

Do you think that if I let go of all of this, I'll fall?

—LADON TO DENNIS, A FEW WEEKS BEFORE PASSING

Like all "threshold" experiences—birth, learning to talk, falling in love, creating art—dying proceeds on its own timeline, off the clock and calendar. Upheld by a committed circle of prayer, love and care, Ladon hung on longer than any of us expected.

One day in mid-July, local crone Karolla Dauber was walking up to the house as she did each morning to do bodywork on Ladon. We could see that she was agitated, and asked what was wrong. "Each day I come here I see the spirits gathered around this place," she said solemnly in her thick German accent. "This morning their voices were so loud. It was as if a great banner was hanging over the house announcing: *A holy man is dying here!*"

But dying is a mysterious process—even for holy people. We often discussed with Tensie and Dennis the parallels between Ladon's process of letting go, and his namesake little Thomas Ladon's struggles to take his first upright steps. Toward the end we imagined the cloud of witnesses cheering Ladon on toward his new way of being, just as we adults were encouraging Thomas. To be sure, Ladon struggled with many aspects of this difficult passage, understandably riding an emotional roller coaster.

And we rode it with him. But in the end he came to a place of acceptance. "Whether or not I am physically cured," Ladon intoned more than once, "I believe the real healing has already begun."

Complicating the spiritual process of dying, however, are the *politics* of the "death-care industry." For weeks Elaine researched green burials, in an effort to lay Ladon in the ground according to his wishes for simplicity and our desires to tend to his body. We agreed with him that nature's intention was for our bodies to be reunited with the earth and eventually to recycle into new life. However, the local mortuary told us that embalming was *necessary* and that the coffin *must* be placed in a concrete vault. Elaine found out that the law requires none of this—and in the process discovered a lively grassroots movement committed to burial that is healthy for the earth, meaningful for the caregivers, and respectful of the deceased.[12]

We decided with Ladon that the local village cemetery was the most practicable place to lay him to rest, given our limitations of land and resources. We then met with the caretaker to explore the possibility of a green burial. An indigenous Chumash man, he had never had anyone ask for this before, and was sure the board wouldn't like it. But he also knew that it was not illegal, and to him it sounded more "in keeping with the old ways." When Elaine broached the subject of Ladon's strong wish that the cemetery's American flag not be flying on the day he would be buried. The caretaker asked why and listened carefully as she described Ladon's commitments. "You know," the caretaker responded, "I think I would have liked your friend."

Elaine gave regular updates to the community on her research, and we discussed dimensions for digging the grave and options for markers. When she reported that dry ice was the best way to preserve a corpse, Ladon quipped, "Elaine, you know how much I *hate* to be cold." As we wondered how we were going to get the body to the cemetery, and how to wrangle it into a grave four feet deep, yet again the right skills appeared just as we needed them. A Mennonite friend from the Midwest made a beautiful pine coffin in the backyard, which we would use to transport the body (but not to bury it); another friend sewed an exquisite hammock strong enough for us to lower the body into the grave.

Ladon's final weeks took on the shape of a vigil, as we stayed with him in turn around the clock. In the end it became what could only be

12. Online: www.greenburials.org; www.greenburialcouncil.org

described as "labor"; indeed, Tensie reflected frequently and eloquently on the similarities between birthing and dying.

On August fifth we gathered for Vespers in Ladon's room and celebrated Eucharist. Early on August sixth—the day we commemorate both the Transfiguration of Christ and the disfiguration of Hiroshima—he slipped quietly into a coma. Twenty-four hours later, his arduous journey of crossing over was completed.

For fifty-six hours we lived with Ladon's body, a powerful time for all of us. The women washed and prepared his corpse lovingly, while the men dug his grave over at Guadalupe Community Cemetery. The hospice room was converted into a chapel, and dozens of people came to pay last respects. We continued to pray around the body, noting how curious and unafraid little Rozella and Thomas were. And of course we wept, laughed and told stories late into the night, a memorial bonfire burning in the backyard the whole time. This was Ladon's final gift to us: inviting us to discover how to embrace in death the radical simplicity and profundity that Ladon had embraced in life.

On August ninth, Nagasaki Day, we laid Ladon's body in the ground with a sunrise ceremony attended by more than a hundred friends. For the first time in weeks, for the exact time of our service, the morning fog cleared. There were some songs, only a few words, and then his body, clothed in his old plaid shirt, jeans and beloved bandana, was lowered— the sling almost but not quite tearing ("Just like my birth canal when I had Rozella," said Tensie). And when we were done, the fog moved back in, covering the newly-planted olive tree at the head of the grave with Pacific Ocean mist. The cemetery flag wasn't raised that morning until long after we were gone.

༒

Empty handed I entered the world
Barefoot I leave it.
My coming, my going
Two simple happenings that got entangled.

—KOZOM ICHITYO,
A FOURTEENTH-CENTURY JAPANESE ZEN MONK

Those words, which hung on the wall of Ladon's hospice room beneath strands of brightly colored peace cranes, became the object of much reflection for all of us. In the aftermath of his passing, those of us who were intensely involved in this experiment have struggled to understand its full meaning. We were at peace about our efforts, knowing we did the best we could. Having put most of our other work aside during this time, we feel now that this was perhaps the most significant work we have ever done.

Still, we have a sense that there is much we have to learn about what we went through. Ladon was our teacher by showing, not telling. We now sense a deeper duty to take care of those who have given themselves to the Way of radical discipleship. And we continue to ponder how to die with dignity in our death culture; marvel at the mystery of how community is shaped; and long to trust more profoundly in the divine economy of grace.

Ladon's absence is an irreparable tear in the fabric of our lives. He challenged us with the fullness of the gospel Way, and was a faithful companion through all the joyful and difficult twists of that Way for decades. Our world is lonelier without him. Yet we are convinced that Ladon's death, like his life, will continue to present a singular challenge and inspiration to our discipleship.

For decades Ladon wove a rich and extraordinary tapestry of witness, relationship and service around North America. His discipleship was not just an example; it was a mirror in which we examined our own faith. His name means "the gift," and indeed Ladon's fidelity to the gospel was a gift to those of us he accompanied. In the end, that gift came back around to him a hundredfold in his hour of need. And it will continue to spread outward as we carry on his legacy in our own discipleship: innumerable ripples in a pond, emanating from one remarkable life.

7

To Die at the Catholic Worker[1]

KIERAN PRATHER

"IT SOUNDS TO ME like you're coming to the Catholic Worker to die." Jeff's comment was jarring, exceptionally blunt, even for the bold Dietrich style; besides, that was not the way I saw it. It was September '91, and I was simply dispensing information to community members who were considering my application to join the Worker. My positive HIV status was no more urgent than the facts that I was a recovering alcoholic and that I belonged to a writers' group. I mean, I was attracted to the LACW because of its work with the poor, its resistance to policies and structures I found offensive, and its sense of community. I did not wake up one morning and say, "Bout time for my AIDS to kick in, so I'd better go off and join the Worker." My death, if untimely, was still a ways down the road.

Then, in December of last year [1992], I was diagnosed with pneumocystic pneumonia (PCP), one of the opportunistic diseases that mark the crossover from HIV-positive to AIDS. All statistics lie, and AIDS statistics lie more than most, but a working guess is that from the initial occurrence of disease, life expectancy is, optimistically, about two years. I heard Jeff's comment in a new way while I was in the hospital, and it seemed he might have been more on target than I had realized. In all probability, I had never stopped hearing it.

---

1. "To Die at the Catholic Worker" first appeared in *Catholic Agitator* 23/2 (1993) 1–2, and is reprinted here with permission. Footnotes and references appear here for the first time.

For the past year, Catherine Morris, another community member, and I have volunteered at 5P21, the county hospital AIDS outpatient clinic, and I have gotten to know patients at every stage of the disease. With one friend in particular, I had the opportunity to walk the journey from good health through bouts of pneumonia, tuberculosis, internal Kaposi's Sarcoma to his death in early January. Whenever I spent time with Edvin, the thought, this is my future, crossed my mind. And so it goes with other patients: when Antonia's shingles spread despite treatment and medication, when Samuel gets over diarrhea from one infection only to get it again from a different infection, I move closer to my own death. "Never send to know for whom the bell tolls; it tolls for thee."[2]

Even at the early stages of HIV disease, some patients respond with depression into despair. In our visits at 5P21, Catherine and I meet people in relatively good health who already plan to commit suicide, "when the time is right," the right time being when the inevitable decline begins, or when the disease becomes too difficult and too painful, or when the patient believes he has become too much a burden to those around him. (The recent "right to die" initiative in California enjoyed a large measure of support in the AIDS community.) In practical terms, it is an understandable response. But not mine.

After recounting the history of a dying priest whose good works were constantly misunderstood by those he served, whose most heroic act is twisted to become grist for criticism and gossip, *Diary of a Country Priest* closes with the death-bed affirmation, "Grace is everywhere."[3] Yet, when life is reduced to practical concerns and pain avoidance, the opportunity to experience grace is lost. If Edvin had chosen to end his life when he started experiencing serious disease, he would have been spared a large amount of pain and suffering. However, we both would have been denied a friendship that was special because it grew in the context of suffering; he would not have known the closeness of his family, from whom he was estranged for much of his adult life. I don't know what will happen to my relationships with my family, friends and community as I move towards death, but I do know that there is grace everywhere in the process.

It is common for people with AIDS to feel cheated, to resent that they are being denied a full life. (Edvin was thirty when he died.) This, too, does not work for me, for each time I play with that fantasy, I find

2. John Donne, "Meditation 17," in *Devotions upon Emergent Occasions* (1624).

3. The 1951 French Film (original title: *Journal d'un Curé de Campagne*) was based on Georges Bernanos's novel of the same name.

myself acknowledging that at age forty-five, I have enjoyed a pretty satisfying life. Have I accomplished everything I wanted to? Of course not. But I suspect that would be my answer if I asked myself the question at eighty. The blessings have easily outweighed the tribulations, and all was framed in the context of varied experiences. I made plans as best I could, only to discover that the road traveled was rarely the road planned, alleys became thoroughfares, and I probably had a happier life because of it. I have few regrets. Along with *The Last Hurrah's* Frank Skeffington, I answer the suggestion that, given the chance, I would live my life quite differently with a strong, "Like hell I would."[4]

Eloy, a nine-year-old boy from Mexico who lives with us at Hennacy House, has sacrificed an arm and an eye to bone cancer—that is a tragedy. A teenaged homie from Boyle Heights takes a bullet in the spine and will be paralyzed from the neck down for the rest of his life—that is a tragedy. That I will die of AIDS in the next two years is not a tragedy. Tragic stories come out of 5P21, but mine is not one of them.

My experience with AIDS has been liberating. I began writing the novel I had planned since high school within weeks of getting my HIV-positive diagnosis. As time passed, I had less interest in career and "planning for the future" and became more concerned with things that captured my interest at the time. Casual interest in things political moved to direct action, protests, and civil disobedience.

Volunteering part-time at the Worker soup kitchen shared equal importance with my office job. There is some truth in the Kris Kristofferson lyric: "Freedom's just another word for nothing left to lose."[5] Long-term goals lost their meaning; each event had to matter at once because there was no spare time. With the diagnosis of AIDS, that attitude is more intense. As John Moore notes: "our confrontation and acceptance of the inevitability of death decidedly heightens our own awareness of the value of life."[6] More than ever, what I do with the remaining months of my life had better be the most important thing I can imagine doing.

I am staying at the Catholic Worker to die.

John Donne tells us, "No man is an island, entire of itself; every man is a piece of the continent, a part of the main."[7] In *Community and*

---

4. *The Last Hurrah*, directed by John Ford (1958).

5. "Me and Bobby McGee," Kris Kristofferson and Fred Foster (1969).

6. Source unknown.

7. Donne, "Meditation 17."

Growth, Jean Vanier spells the same idea out more clearly, "People need companions, friends with whom they can share their lives, their vision, and their ideals."[8] The Catholic Worker was not the original plan, of course; at different times, my choice was to share my life with a wife, then with a monastic community, then with a gay lover. (The road traveled was rarely the road planned.) Nonetheless, communal living in the context of Gospel service and resistance seems to fit my wants and needs today. So here I am, confident it is where I am called to be.

Later in his discussion of community, Vanier speaks of the gifts a new member brings and those that the community gives. At first glance, it is easy to see gifts in terms of talents and opportunities: How can my various skills serve the community goals? What work can I do? However, the true gift is not the overlay of abilities but the offering of self, a presence, such as it may be.[9] In this light, I may have brought to the community gifts of a sense of humor, flexibility, a willingness to try new things, an openness to listening, and to sharing my experiences; but in community, as elsewhere, circumstances change, and the gifts a member offers change.

Two years ago, some of us spent time in the Metropolitan Detention Center as a result of demonstrations against the massacre euphemized as the Persian Gulf War. Our intended purpose was to go to jail to register a moral protest; but as time passed, we began to realize that our true purpose was to be a presence to those with whom we were imprisoned. The importance of the war faded as we entered into the lives of the other inmates. I see the same kind of transition happening in my life again. I came to the Worker because I planned to share in the community's work with the poor and its political resistance. But it turns out that my job is to withdraw from those activities and, instead, show my community how to die.

I don't know how this will be played out, and the community doesn't either. At the current time, the activity is that other members remind me that I have AIDS when I want to carry on as if everything is fine. In a sense, we will shape each day as it comes. Painful diseases loom on the horizon, and I do not do pain well; together we will learn to bear these things patiently. I have internalized our culture's dictum that minimal proof of adulthood is independence and the ability to care for one's self, yet I am moving to a mode where increasingly I will have to depend on

8. Jean Vanier, *Community and Growth: Our Pilgrimage Together* (New York: Paulist, 1979), ix.

9. Ibid., 20–23.

others, perhaps even for the most basic bodily needs. I will probably not do this heroically; the community must learn to give and I must learn to accept. There will be times when my illness might force me to back out of an important project at the last minute; I will have to fight my very human feeling of failure and having let others down, and other members will have to fight their very human feelings of resentment at being cheated and let down. The commitment to community remains unchanged, but the form that commitment takes might change very suddenly and dramatically. Tina Delany, of the LACW community is pregnant, and each community member feels like a midwife as her time draws near. She is carrying "our" child and all of us would be in the delivery room if that were possible. In the same way, the community walks with me on my journey towards death, midwife-ing me into the next stage of existence. It is "our" death, and each community member contributes to it.

The attitude described by Henri Nouwen (in his book *The Life of the Beloved*) is one that I hope to adopt for myself.[10] I look back over my life and see that the choice to join—and leave—a Benedictine monastic community, the choice to live a lifestyle that was positively gay and positively Catholic, the choice to come to the Catholic Worker were not choices at all. They were attempts at vocation, efforts to answer God's call as it came to me in a specific time and place. I do not choose to die of AIDS in my mid-forties, but I accept that as the call I hear today. In the context of my communal living, I want to answer, Yes.

John Donne says that another's death diminishes each of us because we are involved with humankind, and he is right. Yet, from another view, Daniel Berrigan captures the ideal metaphor with *Sorrow Builds a Bridge*, the title of his book on working with people with AIDS.[11] Each person's death can benefit and enrich the lives of those who share in it. Sorrow at my dying from AIDS becomes a bridge linking me with other community members—and a bridge connecting them with each other—in a deeper way. We will become a stronger community as we move through the experience. Grace is everywhere.

10. Henri M. J. Nouwen, *Life of the Beloved: Spiritual Living in a Secular World* (New York: Crossroads, 1992).

11. Daniel Berrigan, *Sorrow Built a Bridge: Friendship and AIDS*, The Daniel Berrigan Reprint Series (Eugene, OR: Wipf & Stock, 2009).

8

May the Angels Guide You Into Heaven[1]

JEFF DIETRICH

KIERAN DIED ON CHRISTMAS morning and with his death we have entered fully into a territory previously explored only at the periphery. For all intents and purposes, death in all its forms describes and proscribes the human condition. Kieran's death on Christmas morning was a gift that allowed us to explore that foreign territory of death and grief.

After Kieran died, Lisa cleaned him up, put him in his favorite Lady of Guadalupe T-shirt, and laid him out in his bed. The entire community gathered to recite the liturgy of the dead that Donald and Sandi put together for all of the deaths that we experience here at our house.

We then canceled our usual Christmas celebration, invited friends and extended community members to come over to the house. For the next fourteen hours we sang and prayed, drank whiskey and cried, ate and exchanged stories around Kieran's bed. In the tradition of a good old-fashioned Irish wake people paid their last respects and said good-bye to Kieran. We closed our soup kitchen and spent the entire week grieving for Kieran.

Before he died, Kieran told us that his death was not a tragic thing. He had indeed come to the Catholic Worker to die. More precisely, he

---

1. Kieran Prather of the Los Angeles Catholic Worker died December twenty-fifth, 1994, at Hennacy House. This article is Jeff Dietrich's eulogy for Kieran, "May the Angels Guide You to Heaven," and excerpts from his article, "Kieran's Mission Fulfilled" both of which appeared in the *Catholic Agitator* 25/1 (1995) and are reprinted with permission.

had come to the Catholic Worker to teach us how to die. Through Kieran we have learned more deeply how to be present to the dying, how to grieve the dead, and how to face our own deaths with courage, dignity and grace.

In our tenderheartedness we recognize that our lives and all of creation are a gift from God, and that try as we might, we cannot control that gift. Our hearts of stone have been transformed into hearts of flesh. In grieving Kieran's death we grieve our own deaths. In facing death we turn control of our lives and creation over to our Creator God.

Even though Kieran Prather was born in Kansas City to parents of Scottish heritage, he always thought of himself as and Irish-Mexican immigrant. This was just one of his many little quirks. He was a man of exquisite taste and sophistication, yet he had the tackiest wardrobe to ever survive the sixties. The man still wore bell-bottoms, love beads, and embroidered work shirts long after everyone else had switched to Doc Martens and Pendletons.

Kieran just didn't fit into any of the conventional categories. So, like Dorothy and Toto he left Kansas (City) at a young age for more adventurous territory.

Kieran had to explore all of the extremes of his personality. From the poverty, chastity and obedience of Benedictine monasticism to the sex, drugs and alcohol of L.A.'s gay bar scene, Kieran was the original "been there, done that" kind of guy.

But perhaps it is only those who have explored their extremes that can find their center. And once he found that center, Kieran never let go because he knew that it included body and soul, spirituality and sexuality, Catholic and gay. Kieran had integrity, wholeness, holiness. Kieran was one of the most centered people I have ever met.

As a consequence, he always had the final word. He could settle the most passionate and vitriolic community arguments with just the right word. For us he was kind of like the tribal medicine man. It was as if he had journeyed to interior regions foreign to most of us, and was able to translate the wisdom of those regions into language intelligible to the uninitiated.

We would be sitting in a meeting trying to untangle some emotional Gordian knot and suddenly Kieran would raise his finger and, with a twinkle in his eye, say, "I don't know what this means but here goes . . ."

Then he would end with, "I don't really have a conclusion for all this." Somehow whatever he said seemed to straighten out all of the knots. Everyone trusted him. He spoke the voice of the community. We called it "talking with the angels."

He could be harsh and critical, but never judgmental. If you wanted absolution or affirmation, Kieran was your man. He was sometimes a little spacey, but that was because he reached a little higher and dug a little deeper into the interior regions of the soul.

Kieran was always late for everything. Meetings, prayers, work . . . he could always be found out on the porch smoking one last cigarette. You might say that the only engagement he was ever early for was his untimely death.

Kieran came to the Catholic Worker to die, and in his death we learn a deeper meaning of our life mission. Just four days before he died, Kieran told us that his death was not a tragic thing, the tragedy is when people die alone and outcast.

As a gay Catholic man, Kieran's mission was to be the presence of the Church—to be the *healing* presence of the Church—to those whose wound was deeper than disease and death. The tragedy is not that people are dying of AIDS—people die all the time. The tragedy is that people die alone, shunned by society.

As a community we have walked the *Via Crucis* of Kieran's dying. Now Kieran continues to walk with us as we carry on the healing mission that he began: our ministry to AIDS patients at County Hospital, our efforts at hospice, our attempts to be church to those who are shunned and left to die alone.

We attempt to create an environment in which it is acceptable to die. To die is human. It is the fear and denial of death that estranges us from our humanity. But while we accept Kieran's death, we also believe that, in some ways, Kieran has not died. His life and his mission continue to be enfleshed in the work of our community.

Kieran is the only member of our community who has ever died. But we know that Kieran is up there now talking to the angels, and we are particularly honored that our first heavenly patron is both Irish and Mexican; Catholic and gay. We just hope that he isn't embarrassing us by wearing bell-bottoms and embroidered work shirts.

On Wednesday, January 11, we buried the ashes of Kieran Prather under a Celtic cross, hand-carved by our friend Karen Roarke. The cross stands in our garden dining area, right near the entrance to our soup kitchen, where Kieran often stood to smoke a cigarette. Joe Prather, Kieran's father, spoke of Kieran having been born at home, and of holding him at birth and how grateful he was to have been able to hold Kieran at the moment of his death as well. We said our final good-byes to Kieran and recited together the Paradisium: "May the angels guide you into heaven . . . "

$$9$$

Who Will Roll Away the Stone?[1]

CHED MYERS

A HOMILY ON THE occasion of Kieran Prather's Funeral Mass, Mission Delores Church, L.A. December 31, 1994.

> And very early on the first day of the week, when the sun had risen, they went to the tomb. They had been saying to one another, "Who will roll away the stone for us from the entrance to the tomb?" When they looked up, they saw that the stone, which was very large, had already been rolled back. As they entered the tomb, they saw a young man, dressed in a white robe, sitting on the right side; and they were alarmed. But he said to them, "Do not be alarmed; you are looking for Jesus of Nazareth, who was crucified. He has been raised; he is not here. Look, there is the place they laid him. But go, tell his disciples and Peter that he is going ahead of you to Galilee; there you will see him, just as he told you." (Mark 16:2–7)[2]

Native American writer Leslie Silko, in her acclaimed novel *Ceremony*, puts the following words into the mouth of an elder:

---

1. Ched's eulogy for Kieran was published as "He Goes Before You to Galilee," *Catholic Agitator* 25/1 (1995) and is based on Ched Myers, *Who Will Roll Away the Stone? Discipleship Queries for First-World Christians* (Maryknoll, NY: Orbis, 1994), 410–12. It appears here with permission.

2. This passage is from the New Revised Standard Version, passages from Mark in the body of the homily are Myers' translations and follow Myers, *Who Will Roll Away the Stone?*, 410–12.

I will tell you something about stories,
(he said)
They aren't just entertainment.
Don't be fooled.
They are all we have, you see,
all we have to fight off illness and death
You don't have anything
if you don't have stories.
Their evil is mighty
but it can't stand up to our stories.
So they try to destroy the stories
let the stories be confused or forgotten.
They would like that
They would be happy
Because we would be defenseless then . . .[3]

Stories . . . This text from Mark's gospel was one of Kieran's favorite stories. We reflect on it now at his request. But it is not addressed so much to him, since he has gone on ahead of us, just like the Risen One. It is addressed to those of us who remain.

Very early on the first day of the week, when the sun had risen, they went to the tomb. (Mark 16:2)

Sooner or later, those of us who try to follow Jesus find ourselves, like those Galilean women, on our way to bury him. It is the morning we awake to that inconsolable, aching emptiness that comes only from hope crushed, from bitter disappointment, from the death of loved ones. This dawn does not ring a new day. It brings only the numb duty of last respects.

It is a terrible moment. But we come to know it as surely as we once knew the moment that launched us on our discipleship adventure. "Come follow me and we'll catch some big fish!" Jesus had said, firing us with visions of the Kingdom of God. "Do you see these great edifices of domination? They will be dismantled stone by stone!" he'd promised.

But that's not how it turned out. Let the record show that Jesus was summarily executed in the interests of empire. Perhaps his vision of justice and love is a dream deferred indefinitely by the Powers, the Powers that were, that are, and it appears, that ever will be. Perhaps, after all, Death prevails.

Yes, we recognize this storyline. We feel it, particularly on days like today. However much we bravely celebrate the life of a departed friend, it

3. Leslie Marmon Silko, *Ceremony* (New York: Viking, 1977), 2.

feels lonelier without him. And in this loneliness the weight of our own experiences of betrayal, of apathy, of senseless suffering seems so much greater. And then there is imperial history that still goes on, swirling cynically around us and blowing right through us: Desert Storm and the AIDS plague and Skid Row. Through it all we are continually tempted to concede that the world cannot really be transformed after all, not personally, not politically. Kieran Prather, pray for us.

They were saying to one another, "Who will roll this stone away for us from the entrance to the tomb?" (Mark 16:3)

So we join those Galilean women on that last, pitiless leg of the discipleship journey, trudging toward the cemetery of hope. What remains is the duty of proper burial. We bring flowers, come prepared to offer last rites, to salvage some dignity before we go rejoin history-as-usual.

Yet cruelly, even this is denied us. The entrance to Jesus' makeshift tomb is sealed shut by a huge boulder. We halt in our tracks, pulled up short. "Who will roll away this stone?" we cry, anguished, to no one in particular. We feel orphaned and bereft. All that is left of our faith, which in better times dares to interrogate every arrangement of privilege and power, is this one, halfhearted question. "Who will roll away this stone?" We feel the weariness of Sisyphus.

This stone is our final ignominy. It was put there by the authorities to certify Jesus' defeat, but for good measure it serves also to ensure our separation from him. We are not even granted his corpse to comfort us in our therapeutic ritual of grieving. We cannot weep over Jesus' casket or muster brave eulogies. This stone blocking our way terminates, without explanation, our discipleship journey. What an abrupt and bitter closure: a stone that we cannot go around and that we cannot move.

But when they looked again, they saw that the stone, which was very large, had been rolled away. (Mark 16:4)

There is, however, one more moment, according to Mark's story, and upon it hinges the possibility of the Christian church. It occurs when with the Galilean women we "look again" and see that the stone is rolled away. Improbably, the gospel story, like the tomb has been re-opened.

Tentatively we move forward—but only to find that our noble mission of mourning is no longer needed. Peering around in the dim light of the cave, we make out the figure of a young man sitting alone, dressed in martyrs' clothes. He is speaking to us.

"Don't be incredulous. Looking for Jesus of Nazareth, the one they executed? He's not here. See for yourself." (Mark 16:6)

We look around frantically, our heads swimming, our hearts grinding to a halt. Don't be incredulous?! Incredulity does not begin to describe our confusion at this inconceivable news, this absurd contention. Is it possible that neither the executioner's deathgrip nor the imperial seal have prevailed? Then as we gasp for air, comes the last word from this mysterious messenger.

"He's going on ahead of you." (Mark 16:7)

Our knees buckle. Here is a prospect we never considered, one too terrible to contemplate. It is an invitation to resume the discipleship journey—the consequences of which we now know all too well. Suddenly, from deep within us, from that unexplored space beneath our profoundest hopes and fears, roars a tidal wave of trauma, ecstasy and terror all at once. We race out of that tomb as if we have just seen a ghost. And so we have. For in Jesus' empty tomb there is nothing but the ghost of our discipleship past and our discipleship future.

Mark's story ends as it began, inviting us to follow Jesus. This is yet one more call to discipleship. It presents us with the most dangerous of memories, a living one; with the most subversive of stories, a never-ending one.

But for us, standing between end and new beginning, is a stone that is *"exceedingly great."* It is a boulder as hard as our hearts, a roadblock of our collective addictions, a landslide of our collapsed dreams, a mountain of excuses why we can't go on. It represents the dead end of history-according-to-the-Powers.

This stone symbolizes everything that impedes the church from discipleship as a way of life. We are paralyzed before it whenever we conclude that Jesus' vision of the Kingdom of God was and is, for all practical purposes, a well-meaning delusion. And as we near the end of history's bloodiest century, the "Old World Order" having just been thoroughly rehabilitated, this is an irresistible conclusion indeed for the First World church.

Such conclusions have led the church to make one of two fatal errors. On one hand we cut the gospel story short and settle for a Jesus entombed, which is to say a heroic martyr to whom we can build monuments. On the other hand we try to append a happy ending on the gospel featuring a Jesus who can justify all the church's imperial apostasies.

In utter contrast to the resigned pessimism of those who worship a Jesus entombed and the manic optimism of those who worship a Jesus enthroned, Mark's story faces our condition squarely. It refuses to rescue us from our moment of truth before the stone. "*Who will roll away this stone for us?*" This is the last question on the lips of Mark's disciples, and it echoes the anxiety of their very first, screamed into the teeth of a storm that threatened to drown us: "*Do you not care if we perish?*" Both cries articulate the primal anguish at the core of human existence—as potent as our fear of death.

Mark's empathy for our condition, his solidarity with our frailty, is surely welcome. Yet if empathy were all his story had to offer, it could hardly be called good news. So alone with its unflinching realism Mark narrates the miracle of Grace. "*They looked again and saw that the stone had been rolled away.*"

But how? Not by our muscle, nor by our technology, nor by any of our Promethean schemes. The verb here expresses the perfect tense and the passive voice—the grammar of divine action. This stone has been moved by an ulterior leverage, by a force from beyond the bounds of story and history, with the power to regenerate both. It is a gift from outside the constraints of natural or civic law and order, from the One who is unobligated to the State and its cosmologies, The One who is radically free yet bound in Passion to us.

Theology has often called this force Grace. Mark would surely agree with Paul, Augustine, Luther and all those who have carried on the biblical argument with Sisyphus and Prometheus: nothing we can do can move this stone. It has already been rolled away for us. We need only have eyes to see it.

"*To look again,*" has a technical meaning in Mark's narrative. The verb is used earlier to describe how his two archetypal blind men regain their sight. It is Mark's master metaphor for a faith that looks more deeply into what appears to be in order to see what really is. We might translate it literally: "to revision."

In this moment of Grace, the weary old story of the world, in which the Powers always win and the poor always lose, is radically "revised." Jesus is Risen!

But where has Jesus gone? The answer is provided by a mysterious young man in the tomb. Friends here today who shared Kieran's love of good writing will allow me a little poetic license here. Let's imagine the young man in the story as none other than our brother Kieran. He is probably smiling that enigmatic smile at us, head cocked, hands animated.

He says: Jesus is not here in the tomb. Nor is he "up in heaven." Nor does Kieran suggest to us that we look inward to find Jesus. There is only one place we can "see" the Risen Jesus. *"He is going before you to Galilee; there you will see him."* So does the gospel story begin afresh: *"Behold, I send my messenger before you who will construct the Way . . ."*

"He is going before you." Jesus goes ahead of the church, undomesticated by our Christologies of entombment or enthronement. Whenever the church abandons this Jesus, it worships an idol. And idols, the prophet Habakkuk reminds us, are deaf and dumb. Only the executed-but-risen-Nazarene can hear our brokenhearted cries before the stone of impediment. Only he can call us to discipleship—as many time as it takes.

"Get up, tell the disciples and Peter . . ." Kieran, this mysterious young man in white, is specifically addressing all of us whose discipleship has ever gotten mired in the great Denial. All of us who warm our hands by the imperial fire in the Palace Courtyard, our allegiances compromised. There is no wayward journey that cannot be redeemed by the grace of new beginnings. To respond to the invitation to discipleship is to join Jesus where he already is: on the Way.

This gospel was one of Kieran's favorite stories. He didn't just read it; he allowed this story to read him. Now Kieran, too, has gone on ahead of us. Their evil is mighty. But it cannot stand up to our story.

PART II

Remembrance and Resistance

10

Day of the Dead and Death Well-Lived

Mary Bradford

I'm not afraid to die.
I just don't want to be there when it happens.

—Woody Allen

We decided to make bagels on that rainy winter afternoon. This was in the days before bagels became as common as hamburgers, so it seemed quite exotic to be with my marginally Jewish boyfriend, setting the dough near the heater and waiting for it to rise, keeping each other warm. I had never tasted a bagel before and life was exciting and just beginning to unfold . . . He was dead before the spring was over.

The dead come back whether we invite them or not.
They are our friends, our brothers and sisters, our parents and ancestors,
our children, our lovers.
They bring memories, insight, blessing and good fortune.
They travel a long, long way.
Who would greet them with a dark house and an empty table?
Show them you remember them. Put out the things they loved,
even the things they loved to death.

Don't be so judgmental. You can't reform them now.
Fill the bellies they no longer have.
Refresh the skin that cracked into a fine husk and drifted away in the desert.
Give the old man his glasses. Maybe he will find his eyes.
Put away your sadness. It sours the music.
Hear the music and dance with the quick, the light, the dry-boned.
One autumn the feast will be for us.

From Chaplain Ray Kelleher's handwritten notes about *Día de los Muertos*/Day of the Dead.[1] Ray was an extraordinary hospice chaplain who died unexpectedly in July 2009.

❦

"Isn't that depressing?"

It's a question I get asked occasionally when I tell people I work for Hospice. Other reactions include awkward pauses, curious inquiries about what it entails, expressions of deep appreciation (usually rooted in someone's personal experience with a loved one's death) and the occasional suggestion that all hospice workers should be canonized as saints. I keep the conversation moving by suggesting that Hospice—and by extension any accompaniment of a dying person—is really *Reverse Midwifery*. Using birthing imagery to talk about death is something that resonates with many folks. To promise a dying person: "I will accompany you as you die, as you birth out of this life and into something mysterious and new," is a challenge to our culture's avoidance of death.

With humble beginnings, the modern Hospice movement slowly took root in the United States about forty years ago, becoming a Medicare benefit in 1986. Dame Cicely Saunders, an English physician, is responsible for introducing the idea of holistic care for the dying. In 1967 she created the first modern hospice, St. Christopher's in London. Dame Cicely didn't believe that people should have to die in pain—physical or spiritual. This holistic approach to death led her to advise physicians to ask their dying patients: "How are you within?"[2] It was a radical notion at the time to suggest that dying people should have their fears addressed directly. Talking openly about death was, and still is, uncomfortable for many.

1. Reprinted with permission from his family.

2. Cicely Saunders, *Cicely Saunders: Selected Writings 1958–2004* (New York: Oxford University Press, 2006).

Swiss psychiatrist Elisabeth Kübler-Ross summed it up nicely, testifying at 1972 senate hearings on the subject of death with dignity: "We live in a very particular death-denying society. We isolate both the dying and the old, and it serves a purpose. They are reminders of our own mortality."[3]

Three years earlier, Dr. Kübler-Ross had written *On Death and Dying*, her classic book based on more than 500 interviews with dying patients. In it she outlined her famous *Five Stages of Dying*: denial, anger, bargaining, depression, and acceptance.[4] This groundbreaking work was one of the first books to openly discuss death and it got people talking. The idea of dying as a process that could lead to growth was a breakthrough and it laid the ground for the eventual acceptance of the Hospice movement.

It's unfortunate that Kübler-Ross' stages have often been interpreted rigidly, as though the dying process could be neatly predicted and packaged. She repeatedly stated that she never intended the stages to be a set framework. Instead they were possibilities of what dying people—and those accompanying them—might go through. Afraid? Shocked? Grateful? Accepting? Angry? Full of regrets? Peaceful? It's all in there. Sometimes people work though this messy mix of feelings precisely as outlined. More often, though, a complex process unfolds that repeats some steps, disregards others, and creates unique steps to deal with whatever is needed.

In Hospice we often tell people that we are there to help them "live well" the time they have left. It's the ultimate paradox: death well-lived.

❧

So there she was, sitting on a log with Jesus—yes, that Jesus. Although he was sitting next to her and their shoulders were touching, she was facing the opposite direction. That's because she was furious at him. A few months earlier she'd been eagerly planning a new chapter in her life. Recent rough times had given way to new opportunities. As a Christian who prayed regularly and deeply, she felt that Jesus had put his stamp of approval on her plans. Then she was diagnosed with Stage IV metastatic bone cancer and just like that, the nightmare began. She soon developed an intestinal blockage that kept her from eating—particularly cruel since she was an organic

3. "Death With Dignity: An Inquiry into Related Public Issues," Hearings before the Special Committee on Aging, United States Senate Ninety-Second Congress, Second Session, Part 1, Washington DC, August 7, 1972, 12.

4. Elisabeth Kübler-Ross, *On Death and Dying: What the Dying Have to Teach Doctors, Nurses, Clergy and Their Own Families* (New York: Touchstone, 1969).

farmer and gourmet cook. She made it clear to her Hospice team that she wasn't ready to die yet, given that she had some unfinished business with the Son of God. She requested artificial hydration so they could have some time to work things out. That's how she ended up on the log. Looking away from Jesus, she found herself scarfing down a big bowl of buttered mashed potatoes—extreme comfort food, she called it. She wanted to be sure he saw what she had lost and besides, it felt good to imagine the food she could no longer eat.

She called this a recurring vision, not a dream, but she couldn't really explain the difference. She just knew that it was strikingly real to her, and she brought me up to date on her status with Jesus every time I visited. They remained in that same awkward pose for nearly two months as she became progressively weaker. He never left her. In the end, she put down the bowl of mashed potatoes and moved to the other side of the log, sitting alongside him, but never speaking to him. Last I heard she was leaning over and looking up at him quizzically as they sat in silence.

She had a very peaceful death.

తఎఎ9

Living death well involves participating in a Holy Conspiracy of sorts. I'm referring to conspiracy in the best sense of that word, drawing on the original Latin, *con-spirare,* which means, "to breathe together." Our conspiring is holy when we consciously and lovingly accompany a dying person, or when we allow another to accompany us in our own death. This breathing together is clearly sacramental—there's no question of its being an "outward sign of divine grace," to quote a popular definition of sacrament. But it is more than that. It is a Holy Conspiracy in that it invites us to come together to acknowledge that death is part of life and as such it should not be hidden or heroically resisted when its time has come. And it is a Holy Conspiracy in the modern sense of the word, too—a plotting, if you will—of a mildly subversive nature that conspires to challenge our death-denying society by saying: We intend to face death openly by living the dying process fully and by honoring our dead through ritual and memory, laughter and tears.

తఎఎ9

Can I do that?

She was hesitant to anoint the body of her love. He had died minutes earlier, just before she arrived for her daily visit. We had been talking for

weeks about the possibility that he would choose to go when she wasn't there
because it might be too hard for him to let go with her at his side. And
so it was that he died peacefully right before she walked in on that rainy
morning. She was tearfully sitting with his body when I asked if she'd like
to anoint him. We had no special oils, only some wonderful smelling lotion,
but it would do just fine. And that's when she expressed her concern that
the funeral home or the staff at the nursing home might be upset if she
did. Certainly the "professionals" had rules that must be followed. She was
visibly relieved when I reminded her of her own power and of her place in
the long line of women who throughout the ages have prepared bodies. She
forgot about the professionals pretty quickly.

We stepped into a holy space together as she gently, lovingly massaged
his body with the sweetly scented lotion, telling stories of how they had met
six years earlier: "two hell-raisers who just happened to find each other." She
laughed and cried and hugged me hard.

Skeletons are everywhere. They push baby carriages, wear elaborately
decorated costumes, dance at weddings, and play pianos in the plazas.
On November first and second the festivities of *Día de los Muertos*/Day of
the Dead are in full swing in Mexico. *Pan de Muerto* (Bread of the Dead)
and *calaveras* (sugar skulls) are prominent in the bakeries and families
decorate graves and set up altars, often setting out favorites foods for
their loved ones. Paths of marigold petals are scattered to help the dead
find their way home since many believe that the veil between this world
and the next is thinner during this time. It is important that the dead feel
welcome when they come to visit.

Indigenous origins overlaid with the Christian observances of All
Saints and All Souls Day make *Día de los Muertos* the most reverent ir-
reverent festival you could possibly imagine. Instead of shrinking away
from death, it is honored and celebrated in a light-hearted, very real way.
The fear of death—which is perhaps the ultimate human fear—is brought
into the open and people dance with it. They also cry with it, acknowledging the pain and loss. It is an affirmation of the belief that this life is
just one part of a mysterious journey that continues on after our death.
To dance with death in this manner implies a trust in a benevolent God,
one who desires that our love and connectedness continue long after our
lives here have ended.

Día de los Muertos is gaining in popularity in the United States, and that's a good thing. We can use a blueprint for how to celebrate the joyful, painful, crazy complexity of death.

❧

"How's a you Daddy?" my grandmother asked with her thick Italian accent as I walked into her room at the nursing home.

Just a few months shy of her one hundred and second birthday, she was changing—getting more confused—and it seemed like her long life was finally winding down.

My dad had been dead for almost a year, so I hesitated before answering, "Oh, he's OK, Grandma."

"Call a you Daddy," she told me.

Not wanting to upset her, I decided to enter into her reality; stepping over to the phone I pretended to call my Dad. She seemed pleased, then told me, "I'd like-a my tea."

It didn't hit me until I had reached the kitchen: she was back in time, reliving our afternoon visits from so many years ago. During my high school days I would often take the bus down to her house after school instead of going home. The ritual went like this: I would walk in, give her a kiss, call my dad so he would know to pick me up when he got off work—and then I would walk into the kitchen to make Grandma her tea, just the way she liked it: weak, with lots of milk.

We'd spend an hour or so together as I did my homework and she fingered her rosary beads. We'd talk from time to time, but mostly we just spent time together. I loved the peacefulness of those afternoons—they were such a contrast to my usual busyness—and there was such comfort in the ritual.

DOPO 38 ANNI DI VITA
MORI IL 22 DI APRILE 1905
TERESINA GRECO
LASCIANDO DESOLATI
TRE TENERI FIGLI
E L'INTERA FAMIGLIA DOLENTE
LO ZIO PARROCO GRECO
IN SEGNO D'AFFETTO POSE

AFTER 38 YEARS OF LIFE
TERESINA GRECO
DIED THE 22ND OF APRIL, 1905
LEAVING DEVASTATED
THREE YOUNG CHILDREN

AND THE ENTIRE FAMILY IN PAIN
HER UNCLE, FATHER GRECO
PLACES THIS AS A SIGN OF AFFECTION

Two years after my grandmother died, I found myself in a damp, dilapidated mausoleum in the cemetery of the southern Italian town she had left nearly 80 years earlier. I had found the grave of Teresina, her beloved mother who died of toxemia in her eighth month of pregnancy. My grandmother was nine years old at the time, the oldest of those "three devastated young children"—her mother's death was a wound from which she would never fully recover. The remainder of her childhood was spent living with "her uncle the priest" and her cousins, her father remained a distant figure for her.

I spent an entire day doing rubbings of that remarkable tombstone. As the hours passed, I began to feel a strong connection with this woman, my great-grandmother who had died so young. And I imagined the heartbroken little girl who stood at this grave so many years ago, weeping for her mother.

I've heard it said that we don't truly die until there is no one left to remember us. So each year, as October turns into November, I remember the dead—my dead. I have no idea if they actually come to visit during that magical time, the days of All Saints and All Souls/*Día de los Muertos*—I just know that I feel their presence, so somehow they do live on in me. I talk to them as I set up an altar and lay out their treats. The conversation varies from year to year, but here's how it went the year we lost Ray:

Grandma Rose (Nonna Rosinella), here's your milky tea, just the way you like it. *Ti voglio bene.*

Tim, bagel-maker and first love, I brought you a new age bagel—they make them in all sorts of crazy flavors these days. You are forever present in the mountain.

Dad, here's a shot of Drambuie and a Lotto ticket (which didn't win—sorry). See you in the stars.

And then there's Ray: still can't quite believe that "this autumn the feast is for him." I don't know what his favorite foods were, but I do know that this is the guy who once convinced a gullible colleague that he was giving up bathing with water because of worldwide water shortages, that he was instead going to bathe only using Purell Hand Sanitizer. He called it the *Purell Full-Body Wash System.*

So Ray, because we still miss your delightfully warped sense of humor, you get a bottle of hand sanitizer. This Purell's for you, my friend!

Back from the Brink[1]

Murphy Davis

MYSTERY AND MIRACLE

The corridors of "Old Grady," Atlanta's aging hospital dedicated to serving the city's poorest citizens, were dark and dingy. Night and day flowed together in barely shifting tones of gray. I do not remember windows, though I'm sure there must have been some.

My eighty-three year-old parents were there, having driven down from North Carolina to attend to their ailing daughter. My sister, Dot, waited with them. My partner, Ed, and our teenage daughter, Hannah, shifted nervously on their feet. The soft rustle of starched white coats moving quickly toward us in the darkened hall stays with me.

Bustled—that's the word. The two doctors bustled through the double doors and down the hall to the family conference room where we were waiting. Their long white coats whispered to announce this meeting as a sharing of "official medical information." Dr. Michelle Spector was in charge, and Dr. Marilyn Washburn moved as close behind her as she could.

Dr. Spector had been called into the operating room a week before in the early-morning hours of March 29, 1995, when I lay splayed open on a surgical table deep in the bowels of Grady Memorial Hospital. The

---

1. A version of this article appears in Murphy Davis's forthcoming self-published book, *Surely Goodness and Mercy: A Journey into Illness and Solidarity*.

first surgical team had found tumors in my upper abdomen and done what excision and repair they could, then called in the ob-gyn team. Dr. Spector removed the larger tumors—including presumably the primary one—and I left the O.R. minus my uterus, ovaries, appendix, and a portion of my ruptured small intestine.

Dr. Spector presented my case at a pathology conference at Emory University School of Medicine, where great minds and hearts were brought to bear. Pathologists, surgeons, hematologists, and oncologists assembled with their reports and collaborated on a diagnosis: "Burkitt's lymphoma." Dr. Spector pronounced the strange words to us.

The grave faces of the two doctors communicated more than the words. As Dr. Spector spoke, her eyes filled with tears, and sorrow spilled its wet tracks down her cheeks. My heart reached toward her. Expecting a cold clinical report, we sat instead with a compassionate young woman who wept with the news she bore about this rare and lethal cancer.

That was the beginning of a mystery that has lived in and with me ever since. It is the mystery of illness and suffering shared in compassion—and then transformed from the unbearable into that which must be, and therefore *can* be, borne. What I recall most vividly as I feel my way back to that moment is that the news came to us as a family. I was never, for one moment, alone.

Ed returned later that night to our home, the Open Door Community. Since 1981, we have shared life in this interracial community of faith that we founded with friends, serving and agitating for homeless men and women and prisoners on Georgia's death row. Ed shared the medical report. From there, the news fanned out—to the streets, to the cat holes of our homeless friends, to prison cells and dormitories, to homes, to churches and synagogues, to monasteries and mosques. Across the city, across the country, and across the seas.

But even before the news spread, the prayers had commenced. And the prayers have never ceased. I can hardly begin to describe what this feels like and means to me. In spite of all the crises and diagnoses and predictions of death, I am alive and well. This is simply a mystery. And a miracle.

PERFECT LOVE CASTS OUT FEAR

The seriousness of my situation caught up with me on Grady's oncology ward. Various doctors had given me survival odds of thirty to fifty percent, predictions of six to eighteen months to live. I pleaded in my journal, "I have come here to fight for the life that I love among the people I love. O, God, will you stay with me?"

My assigned chemotherapy regimen was called ProMACE-Cyta-BOM. "It's going to be rigorous," a doctor told me. "I expect it's about as harsh a chemotherapy regimen as we could give you without killing you outright."

The first chemo drugs flowed into my veins on Maundy Thursday. Holy Week is a defining moment for us each year at the Open Door Community. We hold liturgies each evening at places of significance for our homeless and imprisoned friends. We follow the Passion of Jesus through the week, remembering his final confrontation with the powers of death, oppression, and violence, and the ongoing Passion of Jesus in the suffering of the most vulnerable ones among us.

On the Monday of Holy Week, we always gather on the street in front of Grady. That year, from my hospital room, Ed and I followed the liturgy and were conscious of our friends gathering on the street ten stories below us, as they were of us. It felt more than strange to know that this familiar liturgy was taking place without us—so near and yet so far. But both we and our community carried on with the distinct work that was set before us, and the liturgy enfolded my journey straddling life and death, with the deepest hope for a glimpse of resurrection.

As the drugs dripped into my bloodstream on Maundy Thursday, I thought of my community gathering in front of Atlanta's City Hall that evening to remember Jesus' Last Supper with his friends, sharing the bread and the cup. With them, I had to face my fear head-on. I was assured by the promise of 1 John 4:18, "Perfect love casts out fear." What is perfect love? Was I capable of it?

I was comforted when I remembered that the Greek word translated as "perfect" in this passage more accurately means "mature" or "full." We're reminded at the communion table that in the bread and cup we taste "love in all its fullness." I was struck by the realization that "fullness" is a spatial concept. Love moves in and takes up all the available space, so there is no room left for fear. As the chemo drugs flowed into me, I imagined filling up all the spaces in my body with love, crowding out the fear. The image was reflected in the faces and voices of friends and family who surrounded me with love and care—their love in a very literal way crowding out the fear.

On Good Friday, the community gathered in front of the State Capital to hear the story of the execution of Jesus the Jew, in the place where we also keep vigil every time the state of Georgia carries out a modern-day crucifixion. For me, it was a day of release.

"Welcome Home" signs, balloons, and flowers greeted me at the Open Door, and never did a celebratory welcome look more beautiful to my appreciative eyes.

I did not know then whether I would be cured of cancer. But I did know from the very beginning that I was experiencing healing. In our experience, 910 Ponce de Leon Avenue, the home of the Open Door Community, has been the geography of ongoing miracles, and I knew that I would find one among my loving family and companions.

On Sunday we had our Easter service, as always. I was too weak to join the crowd of homeless friends and volunteers gathered in our front yard. But with assistance I was able to make it out to our second-floor balcony, where I offered the benediction over the throng in my bathrobe. The pope in his ornate robe, delivering his Easter address on the balcony of St. Peter's Basilica in Rome, could not have felt more important or appreciated.

ONE MINUTE AT A TIME

"Oh, this must be *terrible* for you," a friend said to me, "not to be able to do your work." She was one among many who offered such a sentiment of sympathy. But, although I missed being present to the work that was so important to me, and the disease was indeed terrible, I was also experiencing something that was important—and, yes, even good.

I remembered the words of the late lawyer and lay theologian William Stringfellow, who has been a great influence on the Open Door and many other Christian disciples, and who spent many years grappling with life-threatening illness, "My vocation is to be William Stringfellow: nothing more, nothing less."[2] When I had first read it many years before in his autobiography *Second Birthday*, that statement had seemed simplistic. But in the throes of chemotherapy in the summer of 1995, I began to understand what he meant.

My work changed dramatically that summer. I was not driving back and forth to death row. I was not making soup for the Open Door soup

2. William Stringfellow, *Second Birthday*, The Stringfellow Series (Eugene, OR: Wipf & Stock, 2004), 5, 31.

kitchen. I was not writing letters to prisoners or articles for our newspaper, *Hospitality*. I was not preaching or leading worship, providing music or making speeches about human rights at political rallies.

If I understood my work as my vocation, then my illness was a drastic and disturbing interruption. But I came to see that though my work had changed, my vocation had not. The real question for me was: Who am I called to be in this radically changed situation of my life? My vocation was what it had always been: to be Murphy Davis—nothing more, nothing less.

I certainly had no lack of work to do. My days were a full regimen of taking medications, changing bandages, resting, going to the clinic, receiving chemo injections, resting, eating, resting, visiting with friends and family, resting, resting, resting. My work was clearly set out for me, and I was working hard. It took all my energy just to put one foot in front of the other and keep going.

Walking through my illness gave me a profound understanding of what author Reynolds Price aptly called "the moment-by-moment task of healing."[3] My "one day at a time" struggle to move toward recovery from a disease that had attacked my entire physical being deepened my appreciation for my many friends who have found hope in the discipline and patience of twelve-step programs. Sometimes it was a "one minute at a time" journey for me.

THE GIFT OF SOLIDARITY

My first memory of Albertine Yorke is the quick, clicking sound her high heels made on the worn, polished, granite floor. Ed and I had joined other patients, sitting in plastic or metal chairs scattered up and down the twelfth-floor hallway for lack of a waiting room, outside the Grady Hematology Clinic. Still only a few weeks past major surgery and my first chemo treatment, I was feeling none too spiffy and surely had not arrived at the place of thinking straight. But these high heels clicking rapidly across the floor got my attention.

"Ms. Davis?" The voice lilted with a British Caribbean cadence. "My name is Albertine Yorke. I am your social worker."

---

3. Reynolds Price, *A Whole New Life: An Illness and a Healing* (New York: Scribner, 1994), 92. Citation to the 2003 trade paperback edition.

Wait a minute; somebody got something wrong here. My brain struggled mightily to protest. Maybe we should start over, "Hello. *My* name is Murphy Davis. I am a Presbyterian minister. I frequently visit at Grady to accompany and advocate for the poor who are sick or injured, and I often work with Grady social workers. They are colleagues. Co-workers. Peers. Is there something I could do to help *you*?"

Ms. Yorke was unaware of my internal struggle, and she hurried on to explain. "We want to explore whether we might apply for you to be qualified for Disability. I need your permission to speak to Dr. Newcom about this."

Having received my consent, Albertine Yorke hastily turned and disappeared into an examining room in search of Dr. Samuel Newcom, chief attending physician of the Hematology Clinic. I was left in the hall in a state of bewilderment. "I have a *social worker*."

I was medically uninsured and had already cost the hospital thousands of dollars in clinic visits, surgery, and a long hospital stay for recovery. And I was in the midst of a very expensive chemotherapy regimen. Part of the job description of the Grady social worker is to explore any possible avenues for reimbursement from county, state, or federal government programs for Grady's care of uninsured patients.

I was a Grady patient: a bona fide charity case. Funny. I have always claimed to believe that God answers prayer. And it is truth that Ed and I had been praying for at least twenty years—praying persistently and with focus—to find the path of solidarity with the poor. We had asked God to give us the *gift* of solidarity.

Ed and I had moved in December 1981 with Rob and Carolyn Johnson into 910 Ponce de Leon Avenue, a two-story, sixty-four-room former women's mission, to launch the Open Door Community. One by one, in the months leading up to the move and the ones following, we gave up our salaried work in order to devote ourselves more intentionally to ministering to prisoners and creating community with people from the streets.

My salary was the last to go, since I had formed the Southern Prison Ministry and administered the funding, including my own compensation. From 1977 until the spring of 1982, I had assigned myself a salary of $620 per month—an annual $7,440. I had hit, and then forsaken, the highest salary I would ever see. We went on from that time living out of the same funds that we begged and solicited for ministry among our homeless and imprisoned friends.

Until that spring of 1982, we and our children, had very fine health insurance policies. But we began to ask ourselves, How can we strive for solidarity with and among the homeless poor while we hold onto the privileges of salary, health insurance, personal savings, and other such "perks?" Solidarity would have had little meaning if we and the sisters and brothers from the streets with whom we were building community had drastically different resources available to us. So it was decided that all of us at the Open Door would depend upon the care of volunteer physicians, the "charity clinics" with a sliding scale, and—for any extraordinary care—Grady Memorial Hospital.

Health care, in our system of consumer capitalism, is a commercial enterprise. If then one receives it—as I have—and cannot pay for it—as I cannot—one is supposed to feel deeply embarrassed, ashamed, humiliated. Over the years Ed has often said of our life at the Open Door, "We are sophisticated mendicants." Well, now we can forget about the "sophisticated" part. We are beggars: dependents, wards of the state, some of the many "undeserving poor," a "drain on the taxpayers."

The die had been cast with the community's decision to forego health insurance in 1982. The prayers for solidarity had been prayed in the years since. And now I was practically gagging on the fruit.

I had learned by then that Burkitt's, an aggressive form of non-Hodgkins lymphoma, is most common in boys and young men in the low-lying areas of tropical East Africa. The tumors generally occur in the neck and jaw. No adequate explanation was forthcoming for how this middle-aged North American white woman could come up with Burkitt's tumors in her abdomen.

Allen King, a former college professor of Ed's and longtime friend, responded to the diagnosis, "My Gawd! The lengths to which some people will go to be *different!*"

Marshall Handon, a friend and colleague through Atlanta's Concerned Black Clergy, of which Ed and I had been members for several years, exclaimed at a meeting when he learned of my strange "statement of racial solidarity," "Lord, she even got a Black *disease!*"

To be in solidarity with the poor is to experience poverty, and one of the basic realities of poverty is powerlessness. Not having money is one thing; powerlessness is quite another. I was feeling a bit unsure about whether I wanted this gift. Nope, I didn't anticipate it feeling like *this.*

UNDER A DEATH SENTENCE

For years I had preached and written about the threat of death as the common experience of the poor, whether on death row or the streets. By judicial decree, by neglect or deprivation, what we do to the poor is threaten their lives and well-being. I have been on "death watch" with death row prisoners before their executions scores of times, and I have come to see that to be poor in this country is to be perpetually on death watch.

Before the development of modern industrial culture, human beings lived much closer to the daily reality of death—and most of the world's people still do. But those of us in North American mainstream culture live lives of segregation: the young over here in a day care center, the old over there in a retirement home, the mentally ill in institutions (now mostly jails) and the condemned in cells, the homeless under bridges— out of sight and out of mind. We of the upper classes intentionally shield ourselves from those whose suffering might be unpleasant to us. We do not want to watch the deaths of the poor.

Gustavo Gutierrez and other liberation theologians remind us that to be poor *is* to be dying—living every day, every moment, in the presence of death—and in the presence of the threat of death. Before physical death comes, the poor experience the death of health and well-being, the death of power and choices, the death of human dignity, and for many the death of hope itself.[4]

To live in solidarity with the poor is to share this proximity to death. My years on death row and with homeless sisters and brothers had taught me more about death than I ever knew to look for. The prospect of my own death joined the concerns that had become a part of my life, my work, my prayer.

No one was about to kill me. No one wished me dead (well, at least no one had ever said so to my face). The politics of the death I faced were different, but it was no less death. I had been told to expect death from this aggressive cancer—if not soon, then before long.

"You've been with us all these years. Now you really know what we're going through," a friend on death row wrote. "You are one of us," wrote another. "You have a death sentence, too." One friend expressed his hope that I would "get a stay." The cards and letters poured in quickly and

4. Gustavo Gutierrez, *A Theology of Liberation: History, Politics and Salvation*, translated and edited by Sister Caridad Indad and John Eagleson (Maryknoll, NY: Orbis, 1988), xxxiv.

often from death row, bearing expressions of sorrow, fear, love, solidarity. Prayers and fasting were offered and promised.

The good fruit of accompaniment was all around me. I was showered in blessings as those I had been with in prison now joined me on my own perilous journey. Lying in a hospital bed or waiting in a clinic at Grady, I felt a deep communion with my friends on death row—the many who had died by execution or medical neglect—and those on the streets who had died from exposure or malnutrition. The deep and life-changing experience of solidarity with the poor had begun prior to my life-threatening illness, and it was a wonderful resource.

What I felt as I faced my own death was a nondramatic, almost nonchalant, recognition that I had undeniably taken a step further on this journey. I was grateful that I had already been well equipped to walk into this theretofore unknown, and certainly mysterious and grace-filled, territory. A new dimension forced its way into my existence, and it led me to gratitude for every day of life—and, eventually, to a rather calm acceptance of the fact that I will die. And among many friends from the streets and our friends from death row I will be buried in the piney woods in the little cemetery at Jubilee Partners community.[5]

I had noticed this gratitude and calm in others from the very first visit I made to the emergency clinic at Grady. Many Grady patients are elderly African Americans, and they, more than any others, established the waiting-room culture. Their conversations were sprinkled generously with expressions of faith.

"Yeah, honey, I'm feelin' *real* bad, but I *know* God's gonna make a way for me somehow."

"I'm so thankful that God woke me up this morning in my right mind."

"Oh, I'm *blessed*," was a frequent response to an inquiry of, "How are you?"

These—the people who of all who populate our city have the hardest lives—these are the faithful ones whose mouths and hearts are filled with gratitude and hope.

And recipes. Faith and food were the two most common topics of conversation in Grady waiting rooms. ". . .Well, then I simmer all that in some butter with a little salt and pepper, and then that's the best eatin' you gonna find."

5. This cemetery is described in Peter Gathje, *Christ Comes in the Stranger's Guise: A History of the Open Door Community* (Atlanta: Open Door, 1991), 73.

"Baby, don't *give* me none of that stuff outa' can! I cook my black-eyed peas *fresh* with smoked turkey neck. Yeah! That's what I do. And hot sauce."

We had gone to Grady and taken our seats among the poor and disabled, and we found a banquet of praise.

PAIN IS A PLACE

That turned out to be only my first round with illness and hospitalization. Since 1995, I have faced several recurrences of Burkitt's lymphoma, breast cancer, five major surgeries (and many minor surgeries), five regimens of chemotherapy treatment, several intestinal blockages, and a nearly fatal case of fungal pneumonia. Intertwined with my own struggle, at Ed Loring's initiative and with our community, I have participated in probably the most racially, economically and religiously diverse nonviolent action campaign in the Atlanta area since the civil rights era—the fight to snatch Grady Hospital back from the death-dealing policies of profit driven healthcare. As the feminist movement of the 1960's taught us, "the personal is political, and the political is personal." In the past eighteen years, I have often straddled the thin and precarious line between life and death, and there has often been very little distinction between the personal and political.

At times the burden of physical pain felt overwhelming. There have been times that I would sleep in small snatches and wish for the oblivion of sleep when I was awake. I remember thinking of Flannery O'Connor, the Georgia writer who has long been one of my favorites. During her years of struggle with the auto-immune disease lupus, she wrote to one of her friends, "sickness is a place."[6]

Yes, I thought, and *pain* is a place. You go there by yourself. But you need your people to keep the light on and the door open so that you can find your bearings and make your way back home when you're ready.

Intense pain sends you out all alone on a little raft in a great sea inside yourself, and it blurs the world outside your skin. The world marches right on, but what goes on outside of you takes on a strange, far-away character. You look at it all as if from a great distance and often with very little interest.

6. Flannery O'Connor, *The Habit of Being: Letters,* edited and with an introduction by Sally Fitzgerald (New York: Farrar, Straus & Giroux, 1979), 163.

Pain takes us hostage—especially our attention. Enduring intense physical pain requires our full attention simply to move from one moment to the next. I was far out at sea on my tiny bark—hanging on for dear life as the waves pounded over me, threatening to overturn my fragile craft and leave me to drown.

But from time to time I would open my eyes. And I would see—as if through a dense fog—my family and friends. It was as if they stood watch on a distant shore, keeping me from becoming completely lost. I knew that when the time came for me to return, their faithful vigil would help me get my bearings for the journey back home.

Those of us who have suffered such extended and excruciating pain wonder in the throes of it whether it will ever end—and not knowing complicates the agony. We come to recognize the desperate place within us that would do virtually *anything* to end the pain. Thankfully, each of my many episodes of such suffering came to an end. These harsh and unwelcomed experiences have forced into my consciousness and prayers those who live this day with chronic and unrelenting pain.

William Stringfellow wrote that pain is an "acolyte for the power of death."[7] Even when a reprieve comes, the sufferer knows that s/he has experienced a foretaste of dying.

On the positive side, illness and pain can become an opportunity for re-inhabiting our bodies. Bodies carry memory and solidarity with the creation that we often have "forgotten" or suppressed. "Re-membering" ourselves is an opportunity for deepening our incarnational theology— the stunning awareness that God chose to come to earth in the flesh and share our sufferings.

My pain belongs not just to me but to the human family. It can isolate me and make me think only of myself and my desire for relief—or it can become a deep cry from my own depths for the pain of all who suffer, a bridge to others. When I can creep out of my own place of suffering long enough, I see the others who suffer: their faces, tired and worn from their troubles; their brave smiles and faithful thanksgivings for another day of life, for "coming this far by faith;" their confident declarations that "God hasn't brought me this far to leave me now."

Humor has helped me to survive. When you're deathly ill, it's a good idea to surround yourself with people who can help you laugh at yourself

7. William Stringfellow, "The Ambiguity of Pain," in *Keeper of the Word: Selected Writings of William Stringfellow*, edited by Bill Wylie-Kellermann (Grand Rapids: Eerdmans, 1994), 66 [62–66].

and the absurdities and indignities of your situation. This was especially true for me when I hit one my absolutely lowest points.

In July of 1995, I had my second intestinal blockage requiring hospitalization, a result of adhesions—scar tissue—from my extensive abdominal surgery. I thought I was going to die from the pain and vomited for hours on end. As I moved through Grady from the clinic to the Emergency Room to the Radiology wing, I threw up in bags, bowls, and trash cans.

Sitting on the edge of a cold, steel table, I wept when a radiology technician handed me a large glass filled with a heavy, chalky, white liquid and told me I had to drink it—such was the protocol for a barium-swallow X-ray. When you're vomiting green stuff and not really at your social best, it's comforting to be gently assured that barium is so heavy that, no matter how many times you throw up, it will stay put.

A few days later, I was feeling much better and a second X-ray was ordered. Ed helped me into a wheelchair and covered me with a sheet. While I pulled my IV pole along, he wheeled me down the hall to the elevator and on to Radiology on the third floor. The nurses and technicians at the nurses' station greeted us warmly.

After the X-ray, Ed asked me, "Do you feel like you could walk a little bit?" I answered, "Sure."

When I got out, Ed climbed quickly into the chair, wrapped the sheet around his head and shoulders, and grabbed the IV pole, looking as pathetic as he could. I pushed him out toward the nurses' station as if this were perfectly normal. The women at the station did a double-take, looked horrified, and then burst into gales of laughter.

At the time, Georgia Congressman Newt Gingrich, soon to be Speaker of the US House of Representatives, was pushing a plan that would have gutted federal support of healthcare for the poor. As we passed the nurses' station, Ed yelled, "It's the Newt Gingrich healthcare plan: the sick push the healthy!"

The nurses and technicians could not contain themselves and were still laughing as the door swung shut behind us. One ran after us and said to Ed, "You have no idea how much you help us when you make us laugh."

Truth be told, it helped us all.

STICKING TO THE FOOTPATH

During my bouts of illness, I cultivated an appreciation for, and identification with, the story of Jesus and the paralytic, recorded in the second chapter of the Gospel of Mark. The paralyzed man's friends were so determined to get him healed that they circumvented the gathered crowd, tore open the roof, and lowered the man on his mat in front of Jesus. Jesus was so moved by their faith that he healed the man, who picked up his mat and left dancing and glorifying God.

This ancient story has been my story as well. A multitude of dear family and friends have symbolically torn off the roof to carry me to Jesus' feet for healing—not just once, but many times. In my utterly powerless state in the numerous times of critical illness, I could do nothing but surrender to their loving, extravagant care and tireless determination.

As I grew stronger after my first illness, one of the prayers in Michael Leunig's lovely little book *The Prayer Tree* became a constant companion for me. His words speak deeply to me:

> We pray for another way of being: another way of knowing.
> Across the difficult terrain of our existence we have attempted
> to build a highway and in so doing have lost our footpath. God,
> lead us to our footpath: Lead us there where in simplicity we
> may move at the speed of natural creatures and feel the earth's
> love beneath our feet.[8]

My cancer enforced a reduced speed, but I was already beginning to wonder how I would carry this speed limit into the future. In her book *The Alchemy of Illness*, which provided great insight as I cycled through years of crisis and recovery, Kat Duff pointed to the serious dilemma of times of health. The great temptation is to "re-cover": to cover over the time of illness, to forget about it and rush on as if it never happened. But the need for the footpath—the slow pace that allows for remembrance and meditation and time to honor the wisdom revealed in a serious illness—remains.[9]

This is really the hard part. When you've been ill, most people want you to "get back to normal" as quickly as possible. The needs that waited patiently during the illness begin clamoring for attention. How to go forward without falling back into the frenetic pace?

8. Michael Leunig, *The Prayer Tree* (New York: Harper Collins, 1998), pages are unnumbered.

9. Kat Duff, *The Alchemy of Illness* (New York: Pantheon, 1993), 17.

I would never say that I was happy to have had such close brushes with death. But there is no denying that many blessings have come to me that I would not have received had I not gone right to the brink several times and come back. One of those is the hard reminder that without focused quiet reflection and prayer, we run the risk of becoming fragile, brittle, shallow, soul-less people.

I had known this truth before my illness, but I had neglected the importance of it. In the frantic years of activism, resistance, and hospitality work, the needs were just so great that I could always justify to myself rushing on and neglecting the time for pondering and meditation. During my recovery, I realized that the path of least resistance would be to plow back into a full schedule. It would reassure a lot of people. It would help us all to forget that this unpleasant period of my life had ever happened. But this would be another form of death.

While I did not suffer the illusion that I was responsible *for* my own illness (in the sense of "causing" it by something I had done or not done), I knew, as Kat Duff reminded me, that I had to be responsible *to* what I had experienced and learned. And part of that meant living at a pace that was more in tune with the needs of my body and soul. The many changes that my body had gone through had to be honored in some way, and the needs of my spirit and soul required my continuing attention.

God's Spirit rarely shouts from deep inside of us. In our day-to-day lives, the voice of the Spirit within us usually speaks in whispers. We do not hear this quiet voice readily when we are rushing around. So if we act and live only out of the will and rational planning, we miss the depth of life that comes when we are quiet and still enough to hear the important messages of our inner life. Our dreams often speak to us of the ruminations, desires, and attachments of our soul, but the messages are often lost with the morning light because we do not take the time to listen.

How are we to live in solidarity with the suffering and dying poor of the earth without working in a way that is so frantic that it renders our physical and mental health vulnerable to disease and disorders? This is likely to be a dilemma and challenge for whatever amount of time I have left on this earth. This is not just my personal issue; it is an issue that plagues most of us in the activist community. With the notable exception of the many who are unemployed or in prison, the dilemma of frantic activity is a plague of modern life in our techno-industrial society, and those of us who work for something other than money and endless consumption are not exempt.

Grace often comes in strange and unanticipated forms and expressions. And however it comes, we usually resist it. Receiving grace and making the changes that grace might require demand concentration and discipline. Change doesn't "just happen." It is a labor.

The establishment of new regimens of lifestyle, the physical disciplines to enhance the immune system and take responsibility for one's own health, the structured time for soul work—all of this requires focused and relentless effort. It is not something you just "tack on" to an already busy routine. It is an unending learning process and effort. All I have learned to do with it is to befriend the tension and do the best I can in its presence.

Pondering these past eighteen years, I have no formula to share. There is no way to explain why I have lived through the impossible. But I am a living witness to the healing miracle of brilliant, skilled, and compassionate medical treatment combined with the daily reality of being carried through it all by prayer and hope. I have received the tender care of friends and family, nurses and technicians, doctors and hospital room cleaners, co-workers and strangers. I have been buoyed by the prayers of the faithful and the hopes of agnostics, by the persistent petitions of family and the determined conviction of poor neighbors and death-row prisoners.

Let me state clearly that I am alive *not* because I, and those who have helped to carry me, have more faith, or better faith, than others who have prayed and hoped for recovery. During the same years that I have lived through six episodes of critical illness and countless ongoing surgeries and therapies, many friends and family—saints all—have died. Some, including my beloved parents, aunts and uncles, and close friends Patsy, Frances, and Lewis, passed on at the end of long and happy lives. Others, whom I have loved and for whom I have prayed, have had their lives cut short by disease, deprivation, accidents, and exposure—and by electric chairs, gas chambers, and lethal needles.

Why does one person live, and another facing a similar circumstance die? I do not know, and I will not presume to speculate. Some things we can know with something approaching certainty, and some things will forever remain a mystery. As the old hymn affirms, "We'll understand it better by and by."

My task now is simply to celebrate each day with gratitude that overflows for others. As Minnie Ransom, the healer in Toni Cade Bambara's novel *The Salt Eaters*, declared, "Wholeness is no trifling matter."[10] Indeed.

---

10. Toni Cade Bambara, *The Salt Eaters* (New York: Random House, 1980), 10.

12

Digging

Andrea Ferich

Our bodies and the land are one. Move the earth with your body, dance on it, farm in it, play with it; our final return to it is sacred. The soil is made of clay, like you and me—hydrocarbon molecules, layers of geological and muscular formations, alive. The soil, mountains, and valleys are layered with time like our layered muscle tissue. We dance on the earth in the face of death, for the healing of ourselves and the healing of the land, connected as farmers, dancers, painters, musicians, and lovers of the goodness of the good green earth moving through lament. Our bodies and the earth are one and their healing and grieving are interconnected.

January 2011, around the corner from my house, Anjaneah Williams was murdered, across the street from Sacred Heart Church, pierced in the side, at 2 p.m., walking out from a sandwich shop. It was a Thursday. She died six hours later at Cooper Hospital in the arms of her mother, before the children who deeply loved her. One of the gunman's stray bullets shot across the street through the stained glass at Sacred Heart. Anjaneah's death reverberated in the air, an exploding, echoing canyon; a screaming mother in a vacuum, unheard and deafening. Her murder was one of forty in the neighborhood in the near half-century since the shipyard closed. Forty people on the sidewalks, on the lots where houses once stood, in a neighborhood with twenty-eight known environmentally contaminated sites.

Part II: Remembrance and Resistance

Lent is the season before Easter when Catholics make sacrifices and fast with intensified contemplation: repentance, turning again. Forty-four days after the beginning of Lent, a date calculated by the full moon and the Vernal Equinox, is Good Friday, the day that most of the Christian church remembers the death and dying of Jesus. The week before Easter, Christian Holy Week, is honored passionately by people all over the world. The actual death of Christ is reenacted: from the thorny crown to the stripping of the garment and the whipping, falling, beating, hanging. Jesus dying, his blood dripping all over the land. During the ritual of the Stations of the Cross, there are fourteen places to walk to. Each of these stations is another gruesome description of the death of Christ. I've heard of stories of Catholics in other countries almost dying during the *Via Crucis*. The fourteen Stations of the Cross here in Camden, New Jersey, are places where people have been murdered.[1] For some Native Americans *Via Crucis* is also a time when we remember the Trail of Tears. The Trail of Tears and the torture of Jesus were both enforced by a violent empire, a walk of suffering. Walking these stations is an embodied lament, we remember Jesus and the suffering of those who have come before us.

The faithful of Sacred Heart Church in Camden are taught to dance in the face of death during Carnival, the days before the beginning of Lent. This Carnival Sunday Jorge,[2] was introduced to the parish at morning mass. Jorge is ten years old, with huge beautiful dimples. In June 2011, eight months before we met, Jorge was walking to his home in East Camden to change from his school clothes. He was shot in the head, and lost his eyesight when a bullet, intended for someone else, severed his optic nerve. Now Jorge and his family live in my neighborhood with a backyard that connects to the greenhouse where I work. He has his own garden gate at the end of the yard, and he works with us as a Junior Farmer. He is really happy to ride the stationary bicycle in the greenhouse to pump the water for the plants. Jorge's life is beautiful and full of loving friends but I find myself part of Jorge's suffering. He wants to see again, and is sometimes overwhelmed with the terrible meaninglessness of violence. I haven't wrapped myself around the suffering, beauty and meaning yet, perhaps there is no meaning, but I know that I have been deeply moved and healed by this beautiful blind boy.

1. From January to August of 2012, there were forty-four murders in Camden, New Jersey, with a population under 78,000.

2. Jorge Cartagena and his grandmother Manuela want to share his story so his real name appears here. He prefers his name to be pronounced "George."

Carnival Sunday, a poet named Rocky dances all the aisles of Sacred Heart, puppet in hand, dances in the face of the approaching Lenten season.[3] Mardi Gras and *fauschnuts*[4], we dance in the face of death. I describe the scene to my new friend Jorge who keeps asking more questions. I ask him what types of fruits and vegetables he likes to eat.

"Broccoli."

"Wonderful. Jorge, together we can grow all different types of broccoli. You can water them every morning, and you can feel the different parts of the plant—stem, stalk, and broccoli sprouts."

"Oh, yeah, and then I'll eat them."

"We'll fill your yard with the most wonderfully smelling flowers, and special stepping stones to your bench, and a pathway throughout the garden."

He asks me if I wanted to feel something.

"Sure."

He takes my hand and brings it up to his bullet scar.

"This is where I was shot."

He is so open and wanting to tell his story. I ask if I could show him something, and take his hand up to my head.

"This is my nose."

He smiles.

He asks about all of the people around us, the church ladies grabbing his face and kissing him. I touch my hand to the area in his forehead between his two eyes.

"This is your third eye, Jorge. It tells you what is around you and when things are coming, magic like butterflies and flowers in the garden."

He tells me about his parakeets and how he takes care of them, how he loves birds, and we talk about the chickens in the garden. More church lady kisses, and the young children wave to him. He asks about the poet ballet dancing with the puppets in the aisle, he wants to hear the details, of this, our dance in the face of death. The journey into Lent, the death and resurrection, never meant as much to me until I shared it with him. I found a new voice telling the story to Jorge.

We dance and we farm, stay connected in death's deepness, and we find our way toward beauty amidst the violence. This space where the

3. Between the time that this article was written and published, Camden poet and performer Rocky Wilson was attacked and beaten.

4. Named for the German word for Carnival, *Fastnacht*, these donuts were a traditional way to use up fat and sugar before Lent.

children play, kites are flown and orchards grown, this is the space we call home.

Our whispering stops and we listen to the priest Father Michael, the liturgy, the cantor. Singing together our voices rise beyond and within the words we sing, "Lamb of God, you take away the sin of the world, have mercy on us, *grant us peace.*"

I remember singing these words with my grandmother as a small child in her Lutheran Church. A holy woman, gracious and beautiful, I miss her and I am with her when I sing these words in my body. I grew up one block away from her home in Lancaster, Pennsylvania and still vividly dream of that space, the architecture, the garden, flying from her rooftop. Children from the neighborhood would come to the house to hear her sing and watch the glass on the storm door shake as she made her way around the octaves. *Grant us peace.* I grieve and mourn her loss in the emptying and the filling that remembering creates. I fill my body with her singing.

The day before she died, I awoke with a terrible back pain. The pain was telling me to go and drive to Lancaster. I went and sat with her, rubbed her feet, and talked about the beauty of the ocean. I held her hand and told her that she lived and loved a good long life, she would most certainly journey well. I sat with her in silence as she floated, prayers on slowing breath, hearing a new song more clearly. I was given the gift of being with her as she was passing, as her spirit was lifting.

She died and I know she is still with me. Riding the evening train to the field, lanes fade in the hovering dusk. I sit up startled to see my grandmother's face looking back at me, in my own reflection on the train window in the rolling Lancaster landscape. I look down and see her hips, hands, her frame, my body as her dress form. I wash my hands with the last remaining bar of Dove hand soap I inherited from her house. Most of the farmers in the neighborhood have washed their hands with it now. We planted flowers in the garden to remember her. Her children, sisters, and cousins stood beside her grave as she was lowered into the earth on the Lancaster hillside.

Most of the ancient world buried and burned the remains of their loved ones. For most of the 2,500,000 years humans have died, we have returned to the earth, making it sacred across religious perspectives. Many of those who came before us have dug the graves of their loved ones.

Father Michael Doyle, the Irish farmer–poet–priest of Sacred Heart Church is of the earth. He was raised full of the earth's wisdom, its rhythms, the dependency of people on it, and how it remembers. Father Doyle, weathered in seasons, ways of knowing, intuitive farmer, story-telling, touching something familiar and wise. In Ireland, when Father Michael was young, family and friends would dig peat out of the bog to keep the hearth fire going. When it was time to bury a loved one, they prepared the body and dug the grave, to bury their dead in the earth or to return their ashes. They met in the field to dig the grave, a physical act, the spiritual work of moving the earth.

Father Michael's best friend died this year, Joseph A. Balzano, a maritime man, director of the South Jersey Port Corporation's international waterways. A man measuring in tonnage, with his wherewithal, his kindness and his front-end loader, he moved tons of beauty into the neighborhood: statue, fountain, bolder. He donated and leveled the land where the greenhouse and gardens now stand. Joe died this year; we are grieving him and we remember the many times he was a godfather to the neighborhood. Father Michael deeply grieves the loss of his best friend. He really misses Joe, and I asked him about it one time; I asked him how he was feeling. He told the story, "In Ireland when you lose one of your own, you meet with the others in the field with your shovel, to do the digging. We didn't do this for Joe, we didn't dig his hole, and I don't know how to grieve him."

The act of digging the burial hole is sacred, is part of the mystery of mourning. Grieving has a physical side; what is done to the earth is also done to you, moving through the layers of pain.

We broke three pickaxes digging the holes to plant the fruit-trees at the edge of the neighborhood near the river. At this place the earth groans where a murdered woman's body fell. Dawn McCarey was murdered here, her body thrown on this hard and frozen land December 23, 1997. On this land near the Delaware River we walk the *Via Crucis* to remember Christ falling, over and over again on his way to death. Our orchard, *Finca de Ancona*, is one of the Stations of the Cross, one of four-teen sites here in Waterfront South where people have been murdered: shot, strangled, beaten, stabbed. I never knew Dawn McCarey, some-body's daughter, strangled and dumped, found dead in the back alley be-tween industries and families, thrown like weeds not going to seed, land and body unwanted, waiting. We dug and we dug; we broke three pick axes digging and caring deeply, loving the goodness of body in earth. The soil anointed with air, sunlight, and water into fruit and wildflowers. This is our orchard; this is our promise of the fruit trees in the city beside the river, healing the nations, growing hazelnuts, apples, peaches, pears, and cherries. We care for this place, make it more beautiful, and continue to dig our holes. We remember; the earth is part of our Body. May eternal rest be granted unto us and perpetual light shine dancing on.

13

Love Letters
to the Dead Not Worth Saving

Laurel Dykstra

I STARTED TO DO the math. Since 1992, when I first moved to the Catholic Worker, I've prayed at more than one hundred street funerals, memorials, and vigils. Sat on cold metal folding chairs in cheap funeral homes, community centers, and the common rooms of Single Room Occupancy Hotels, in groups as large as two hundred or as small as three, to remember the lives and mark the passing of this society's least loved. Alcoholics, homeless veterans, sex offenders, crack dealers, junkies, transgender sex workers, thieves, cripples, schizophrenics, scabbed, and bad smelling. Who died by suicide, overdose, murder, disease—and none by old age. Where I live people die so young you are eligible for seniors' programs at age 45.

I go to these memorials because I can—because I live a little bit distant from the relentless rising numbers of the dead. I am closer to certain than many of my neighbors that the next funeral won't be mine.

I pass a friend on the street and ask, "are you going to Johnny's service?"

And the answer comes back, "I can't go to those things; I hate funerals, there's just too many."

And really, one hundred's not so many, in twenty years, if you're a hospice worker or an oncologist. But I'm not. I've gone from being a volunteer to a service provider, then a community organizer and now

I'm just a neighbor, not even a very friendly neighbor, and each funeral was a face I knew (I've forgotten so many), a name even if it was a street name—Dollar Bill, Cowboy, Dee—and at least some fragment of a story.

As we sit and listen or pray, I am repulsed by the funeral urge (mine and other preachers') to talk about these "problem dead" as babies, as once somebody's child, as if their adult lives need to be erased and negated. As if they need to be reduced to something big-eyed, blunt, and helpless to remind others of their worth and value. Well, they were valuable as they fucking were—hurt, damaged, dangerous, surviving, living.

Sometimes I can go months without getting a call, "Did you hear about Terri?" or seeing a poster on a lamppost; but sometimes, when I worked at the drop-in center or the drug user group, there were months when I heard about a new death every few days.

During one of those months I was talking to a friend, minister to a nice middle-class church.

"I'm feeling kind of low—three women that I know from the neighborhood have died. But one especially is sticking with me."

"So you're grieving?" he said.

I hear that word and it's like a cartoon light bulb over my head—or more like an explosion. I want to take the word in my hands. It's not just how I feel or what is happening this month, grieving is the word that defines me, maybe for a lot of years now. My role as this silent bystander on some horrible parade to the grave is grieving. It is the work that I do—for people who are not grieved elsewhere. I pray for the dead not worth saving.

My friend is a genius for giving me this word. I *am* grieving. It's like he's named my secret name.

And then he asks, "Did she die violently?"

The genius evaporates and I feel like he hit me. I am struck dumb by the utter inadequacy of the question. The complete failure to understand.

No—Fern and the others were not stabbed, or shot or thrown from a window (although I've been to those memorials too). They died of cancer, AIDS, and heart and organ failure after years of hard living, but all three of them were aboriginal women, under the age of 50. All three lived with the pervasive violence of colonization—land and language theft, sexism, poverty. Even when she wasn't being pinned down for sex by a teen-age half brother, watching her children apprehended by the ministry, trading a blow-job for a rock of crack cocaine, serving jail time for stealing food. Even when she was laughing, telling a joke and sharing a smoke; holding a grandchild; sitting in the sun on a park bench—violence was part of her life.

But the hundred, or hundred and fifty, or however many deaths it is, they add up—if they were coffins standing end to end they'd run a city block. Of course around here mostly poor people are cremated, it's cheaper. So what about those little cardboard boxes, with the body dust all sealed up in a tough plastic wrapper? One hundred would make quite a stack, fill a cupboard maybe or a closet.

So this writing is a little like coming out of the closet. For a long time I've been silent, a mute witness to the rising tide of bodies around me. For so many people in this neighborhood and others where I've lived, their stories are the last thing they have—and journalists, researchers and photographers come to take even that. Posing people against the backdrop of syringe-littered allies. Telling a story to serve their own agenda. My friends, the last thing I want to do is take from you but I'm angry all the time and think I need to speak.

I get caught up too with ideology and race and class and privilege—and what is mine to tell? A white woman with a number of escape routes and a book I can write this story in. Race especially, writing about death means writing about race. Aboriginal people make up about three percent of the population of Canada but here are the names of aboriginal people who I know who died before fifty. In my neighborhood. In the past few years: Veronica, Fran, Fern, Laurie, Noah, Duane, Bobby, Norma Jean, Patty, Marilyn, Mary, Hazel. Just the ones I knew, just in my neighborhood.

I don't know what's mine to tell and I don't know if I will get it right so I am writing to a few of you who I counted as friends—not clients or guests or members (euphemisms that accentuated the gulf between us). Friends, with a friendship that resembled us: tentative, flawed, and bearing too much, but real and good.

I write knowing that what I tell is only a part of your story, knowing that you talked about me too and that I might not have liked all the things that you said either. And that if you were here and you didn't like it you'd say so, and we'd work it out.

So up front my friends, I would not, will not, ever use you as a sermon illustration, poster child, or an object lesson—my agenda is this: less dying, more love and in the face of so many deaths, more outrage. I hope these letters are a gift and not another thing taken from you.

Dear Fern,

I think the first time I really noticed you, was when you borrowed twenty dollars to get back home for a funeral. I know this would piss you off, but before that I would get you confused with Fran and Flo. So when a few weeks went by and you hadn't paid me back—I didn't have twenty bucks to spare—I told you I was starting to avoid you and feel bad about it. You whispered, "Oh, don't do that." I was so glad and we made a plan for two bucks a week and stuck to it until neither of us cared. We did ok across a pretty huge divide.

People would joke that you were always borrowing money to go home to the island for a funeral, and it would have been funny if it wasn't true. I don't know how many aunts and cousins and siblings you lost. I know you didn't go to the residential school but I think about how many of them did and how it impacted you.

It's funny that we got to be friends at all—both proud and shy. Remember how when we were doing interviews for the research project you would cover up the recorder because it embarrassed you so much?

I think of you every time I put on that green shirt from the youth HIV educators. It had been in the office for a couple of weeks and I wanted it but was checking with everyone else first. You rolled your eyes and I'm not sure if you meant, "Why would anybody want that?" or "If I wanted it, it wouldn't have been here for two weeks," or "It's a free T-shirt take the damn thing." Dark green, men's cut, it was not so much your style. You favored short-sleeved cotton shirts, with a small floral pattern. They were faded with washing, with a cardigan over top. I remember how your teeth were always dirty but you clothes were clean.

Fern, I see your girls sometimes downtown, you loved them so fiercely—Angel and I think the middle girl—she comes downtown and sells something with her boyfriend, weed I think, I hope that's all. But she looks good—not skinny or sick and she doesn't stick around long. I smile but she doesn't recognize me.

The older girl with the kids I never see. I know how it hurt you when her husband would hide money and valuables when you came to stay. The stupid shit, when you stole stuff it was so you could bring things to them. Have something to give.

Hey, you know that guy at the club who talked such shit about you for stealing sandwiches and a juice box? Well, he got caught stealing a couple thousand from the membership!

I see Angel more often, it's pretty bad. You know she uses every day and she has to get her boyfriend to shoot her up?

At the friendship center for your memorial all the women were looking away when G talked too long and cried—when we all knew how he hit you. And Angel's dad was there the one that started her shooting dope.

Fern I miss your soft voice and your quiet rage. Like an ember under ash.

Dear Larry,

Getting ready to write this I've been talking to old friends—I called Michael the other night, I remember how he sagged and crumpled when I came to his place that morning and told him you had died. He had forgotten you loved golf. Can you believe it? Well, I guess you could believe Michael forgetting just about anything. But do you know what I had forgotten? Arriving at the cemetery to find Carol chipping golf balls into your grave. Julie remembered that.

Me, Carol, Julie, Mary, Amy, the barrista at the coffee shop, and all the other women you were tragically in love with. You loved smart and young and really, you lived two worlds: Larry sober and Larry drunk. Sober you would talk about books, history, films—erudite, well read, loving ideas. Drunk you would stand swaying, backlit in the long hallway, bearing gifts like some glassy eyed Magi: plush stuffed animals, or tall latte's unaware that half had spilled down your front staining that pale blue jacket.

Do you remember the movie we saw at the art house theatre? The Chinese film about the peasant woman investigated for killing her husband with rat poison? You went out to buy popcorn and never came back—I think you couldn't find our row in the dark--and I stayed to the unsatisfying end, determined not to waste your money.

I think about all those boiled turkey carcasses we stripped for soup, standing for hours over the stainless steel sink. They stank so bad. And how if you were in the kitchen you had to be in charge no matter whose name was down as cook. Both of us stormed off at least once, leaving the other to finish cooking lunch for two hundred.

At the cemetery the grass was green and slick—was it spring when you died? There were only four of us to carry the coffin—Scott and either Michael or Kevin, and a man from the funeral parlor, all standing over six foot, then me. I was at the back on the right hand side as they slid the coffin out of the hearse—it was pale blueish grey with some raised floral pattern— you would have hated it. When the coffin was clear of the car I staggered and slipped on the wet grass. It was the first time I felt the full weight of a body—and Larry, you were a big guy—tall with a serious belly when you weren't too drunk to eat.

Near the grave was a big cedar tree with a crow cawing at the top. I thought it was kind of symbolic and spiritual and you would have liked that but Carol pointed out the constant roar of traffic from the highway how you hated noise.

I hope you're resting in peace Larry, but I hope you're railing against the traffic too.

Milton my friend,

I'm always going to wonder, was there something you were trying to say, something I missed, or that I should have said? You asked if we could talk privately in the chapel. With some guys your age--our age then, it was a request that made me suspicious, a chance to monopolize my time, to be alone with one of the female staff—guys would manufacture vague dilemmas or babble self-important philosophy. But I never got that vibe from you. You were always friendly, non-threatening, the brown kid with the Latino name, "mixed" you said, who hung with the crowd I think of as the dirty white boys. They liked to play spades, get high, and brag about stupid fights. Usually in the winter at least someone had a place, so like a feral pack, forming and reforming depending who was fighting with who, they were in and out of shelters, tents, girlfriends' places, jail, parents' couches, and squats. Zipping ahead in a beat up wheelchair or ambling behind on bent legs, you were everybody's sidekick. The only face you showed was smiling, but I wonder how much of that cheerful hostility-deflecting was personality and how much was finely honed survival skill taught by a world that does not love brown and poor and crippled.

I probably said goodbye at the end of the day, but those few minutes in the chapel is the last time I know we spoke. Two days later you were dead. Suicide. I can't remember who told me, how you died, or if I ever knew.

In the chapel, I got you some adult diapers—we put them in a garbage bag. And we talked about—I can't remember. God, I'm sorry. Something about "life" maybe? Nothing that made me think, this kid's in trouble. Was there something I missed?

But maybe all you wanted privacy for the diapers.

Did you know, for your memorial—the dirty white boys came? Decked out in black denim, belt buckles, chains on their boots. The girls with teased hair and lots of make-up, they'd made an occasion of it. Drunk or high—glassy eyed and laughing and falling into each other. Eyes glittery with tears, makeup and who knows what. They came on the wrong day.

I know now, we should have figured out how to have a service right then—they didn't come back. They'd gotten themselves together in one place, dressed in their best, not fighting, to parade by, to pay their respects.

I am trying to pay mine.

Laurie,

I knew you the least but you are probably the hardest to write to.

We told jokes at your memorial at the women's center—bad jokes, the kind you told:

"What's a thumb tack?"

"I don't know, what?"

"A Smartie with a hard-on."

And long complicated one about a flea transferred from host to host in the hair on various body parts of animal film stars and country and western singers.

Everybody knew you, you walked around the neighborhood like a politician, joking, throwing fake punches and telling stories, you got some kind of response from everyone. A walk around the block could take an hour.

You spent some of your last days at the Tent Village during the anti-Olympics protest tending the sacred fire, talking, singing, telling jokes. I was there too, some. But damn it was cold, February, and wet. And you so skinny from what you used to be. Human interaction must have kept you warm, cause the fire was small, the coffee lukewarm and there was no fat on you. I don't know how you did it.

I don't know how your girlfriend is doing, or the little ones, you were smart, I think, to move them out of this part of town.

I miss you. We never talked a lot, just a "hey" and the butch nod, but I was so glad you were in the world. When I saw you, I would think, "yeah." Fat, loud, laughing, in everybody's face, making no apology for any part of your self. Nothing about you curled up, or hidden. Taking up space like you deserved it.

I was mad when you died. So mad.

Afterward, I was praying and I dared Jesus to show up. "Where the hell are you Jesus, when women keep dying all around me? You better have something to say for yourself."

I was walking around in the rain, bare-headed and crying, Laurie, when Jesus finally showed up it was you. And you were laughing.

Jesus is a drug-user, Native, dyke with AIDS and her girlfriend sells sex—Joke's on me! Because really, who can I tell about when Jesus came to me, without sounding like I picked through every stereotype I could think of for the ones that would piss off religious conservatives the most?

Good joke, Laurie.

I'm leaving his letter with some tobacco in the empty lot where the tent city was.

Fern, Larry, Milton, Laurie, I love you, I miss you. I know I have failed to show you as beautiful and terrible as you were. I don't have a conclusion. I just want someone to know, others to see and care that beautiful, precious, ridiculous people are dying by the hundreds.

And you, whose secrets I said I'd keep? I'm keeping them still. I have not told. I would not use you, or at least no more than you used me.

For these thy servants departed this life in thy faith and fear; beseeching thee to give us grace so to follow their good examples, that with them we may be partakers of thy heavenly kingdom. Amen.

14

Secondlines[1]

JORDAN FLAHERTY

NEW ORLEANS IS INCREDIBLE, glorious, vibrant, beautiful, and difficult. It is a place where life feels more intense, but also more fragile, than anywhere I've ever been. It is a majority-African American city where resistance to white supremacy has cultivated and supported a generous, subversive, and unique culture of vivid beauty. It is a destination with its own culture and traditions, alien to the rest of the US, that nearly everyone who lives here immerses themselves in. From local jazz, brass band music, and bounce hip-hop to secondlines, Mardi Gras Indians, jazz funerals, and a longstanding habit of red beans and rice on Monday nights, New Orleans has nurtured and cultivated its own art and music and food and traditions and sexuality and liberation.

Central to the local culture is the way in which New Orleanians claim the streets. This is a city of porches and balconies where much of the year people decide it is too hot to stay indoors. It is a place where many people know everyone in their neighborhood, and kids traditionally had everyone on the street looking after them. It is a place of barbeques and block parties and—most crucially and uniquely—secondlines and jazz funerals.

The tradition of secondlines evolved from jazz funerals. Today, every jazz funeral has a secondline, but not every secondline is a funeral. On the most basic level a secondline is a parade with a brass band where everyone

1. A version of "Secondlines" first appeared in Jordan Flaherty, *Floodlines: Community and Resistance from Katrina to the Jena Six* (Chicago: Haymarket, 2010), 7–9.

from the neighborhood is invited. The name secondline comes from the formation for a funeral procession (originally from church or funeral home to cemetery): the family is the first line, the band and everyone else is the second line. Hundreds of secondlines are held in New Orleans every year. Sometimes there are just a couple dozen people, crossing a few blocks; sometimes there are thousands of people, three or more brass bands, traversing several miles over the course of four or five hours. Social Aid and Pleasure Clubs, Black community institutions that originated during the Reconstruction era, put on secondlines nearly every weekend, but anyone can throw a secondline—all you need is a brass band. If you travel more than two blocks, people will come out and join you.

The city has more than forty Social Aid and Pleasure Clubs, and each club designates one Sunday out of the year to throw a parade. The Sunday secondlines start at noon or 1 p.m. and each takes a different route, but the majority travel through the African American neighborhoods of either Central City uptown or the Sixth and Seventh Wards downtown. The members of the sponsoring Social Aid and Pleasure Club are at the center of the parade, wearing matching outfits—occasionally changing uniforms once or twice along the way—and dancing the entire time. If you are walking down the street and you see a secondline coming, it looks like a flood of people that will sweep you away, washing over every part of the street, sidewalk, and even the front porches of houses with an ecstatic energy.

At every secondline, a few folks pull watercoolers filled with beer, soda, and water for sale, and along the route people are barbequeing food—sometimes for sale, sometimes just for themselves and friends. Although police officers clear traffic in front of the parade and follow behind, the area within the parade feels like a liberated and communal utopia, where people can smoke pot and drink and lose themselves in music and friends.

Historian Ned Sublette once observed that, "A second line is in effect a civil rights demonstration. Literally, demonstrating the civil right of the community to assemble in the street for peaceful purposes. Or, more simply, demonstrating the civil right of the community to exist."[2] The Social Aid and Pleasure Clubs are exactly what their name implies—societies dedicated to supporting their community and facilitating these public celebrations. Through those gatherings, they help perpetuate this culture and

2. From a mass e-mail sent by Sublette, June 5, 2009.

pass it down from generation to generation. Most of these organizations arose as mutual aid societies in the late 1800s, and much of their purpose lay in providing basic needs such as burial insurance for their members. By upholding this mission of supporting and uniting their communities, the clubs are a large component of what makes New Orleans unique. Through the parades that each club throws, they transform a revolutionary act—taking control of the streets—into something everyday.

Jazz funerals have a more solemn edge, but because New Orleanians observe the death of loved ones by celebrating their lives, a jazz funeral still has the feel of a street party. It can be small—made up mostly of friends and family—or have thousands of people, which is the case when a local musician or other cultural leader has passed away. New Orleans has the highest murder rate in the US, so sadly we have more than our share of opportunities to mourn lives lost far too soon, and far too violently.

In the New Orleans Black community, death is often commemorated as a public ritual, and the deceased are generally memorialized not just through secondlines, but also (as is the case in many other cities, especially in the US south) through t-shirts with their photos in designs celebrating their lives. Worn by most of the deceased's friends and family, these t-shirts remind me of the martyr posters in Palestine, which also feature a photo and design to memorialize a person who has passed on. In Palestine, the poster's subjects are anyone who has been killed by the occupation, whether a sick child who died at a checkpoint or an armed fighter killed in combat. In New Orleans, anyone with family and friends can be memorialized on a t-shirt. But a sad truth of life in exploited communities around the world is that too many of those who passed on lost their lives to violence. For both New Orleans and Palestine, outsiders often think that people have become so accustomed to death by violence that it has become trivialized through T-shirts and posters.

While it's true that these traditions wouldn't manifest in these particular ways if either population had more opportunities for long lives and death from natural causes, it's also far from trivial to find unique ways to celebrate a life. Outsiders tend to demonize those killed—especially the young men—in both these cultures as thugs, killers, or terrorists, and imply that they shouldn't be memorialized in this way (or, often, at all). But the act of commemorating death in this way emphasizes that every person is a son or daughter of someone, and every death should be mourned, every life celebrated. In short, both cultures celebrate life, while they are accused by outsiders of glamorizing death.

One of my favorite holidays of the year doesn't show up on calendars outside New Orleans. It's the last Sunday in November, when the Lady Buck Jumpers, the wildest and fiercest Social Aid and Pleasure Club, takes to the streets. (Some S&P Clubs are all men, some are all women, and some are mixed. Some clubs are all young, some are all older, and some have members ranging from eight to eighty.) Based in the Gert Town neighborhood, the Lady Buck Jumpers are a strong, powerful group of women who dance harder and better than any other secondline crew. The Buck Jumpers' annual parade is always one of the biggest of the year, with thousands of people crowding the streets, dressed in their most fabulous outfits and dancing like it's their last day on earth.

In 2006, the club wore matching camouflage suits in honor of Soulja Slim, a legendary local rapper who was shot and killed on Thanksgiving Day of 2003. As Buck Jumpers president (and Soulja Slim's mother) Linda Porter described it, "The ones here are jumping for the ones gone and the ones to come."[3] This sentiment describes beautifully the spirit of secondlines and jazz funerals, the passionate dancing through tears that I have so often seen.

At global justice protests and other demonstrations, people frequently chant, "Whose streets? Our streets!" And at those gatherings it can feel like a new world is being created simply through the reclaiming of public space as a liberated zone. Activists display a festive spirit that challenges the isolation and violence of capitalism and warfare by showing a vibrant alternative. In New Orleans, on every Sunday, we show that an alternative is possible. And it's beautiful.

3. Nine Times Social and Pleasure Club, "Coming Out the Door for the Ninth Ward" (Neighborhood Story Project, New Orleans, 2009).

15

Breaking Silence
Resisting the Power of Death

ELIZABETH NICOLAS

For to survive in the mouth of this dragon we call america, we have had to learn this first and most vital lesson—that we were never meant to survive. Not as human beings.[1]

—AUDRE LORDE

I AM A BLACK Haitian American woman alive in a culture that wants me dead.

For as long as I can remember, my race, my ethnicity, my gender, my worth, my value, my intellectual capacity, my credentials, my person— my identity really—has been challenged, questioned, degraded and demeaned. Sadly upon encountering challenges, particularly to my blackness and femininity, I have been told (explicitly and implicitly) to try harder, to somehow overcome the presumption against me, to win the challenger over with academic achievement, professional accomplishments, charm,

---

1. Audre Lorde, "The Transformation of Silence into Language and Action," in *Sister Outsider: Essays and Speeches by Audre Lorde* (Freedom, CA: Crossing Press, 1984), 42 [40–44].

by conforming, by assimilating, by self-negating—submitting to the male ego, being "nice," by being "less black."

Even if I am found to be "useful" or "worthy" (helping boost diversity numbers; helping white folks feel less guilty or cool because they have a black friend; standing by my man no matter what), my value is not inherent; it must be earned and it can easily be lost.

My dark beauty is not celebrated, my strength is viewed as a threat. I have inherited legacies of destruction, violence, self-effacement and death. Black slavery in the US and Caribbean. Jim Crow/segregation. Historical and current denials of educational and employment opportunities to black people and women. The prison-industrial complex which like slavery has harnessed the energy and life of the black body. Oppressive eroticization and lyrical degradation of black women. Female body parts and sexuality used to sell products. My hair relaxed when I was nine—considered pretty when straight, ugly and unprofessional when natural. I carry these legacies in my mind and body.

In a society that displays unmasked hatred for me, I have been taught to hate myself, to put myself last. I have been taught to scorn other black people—blame them for their "predicament." I have learned to scorn other women—spitefully compete with them for the heterosexual male gaze. The preferences, the needs, the desires of white people, of men come before mine.

The depth and extent to which I had internalized these lessons came with startling clarity at the end of a destructive relationship with an abusive partner, Billy.[2]

After my first coffee date with Billy, I thought I had met my match; someone who had the capacity for deep thought and conversation, someone who was committed to pursuing justice. I was excited and attracted to Billy's differences. He was white and had grown up in the Pacific Northwest in predominantly white communities. I was raised in Queens, New York, one of the most diverse places in the country. He was conservative, introverted, reserved; where I was liberal, extroverted, flamboyant.

It became quickly apparent that where I viewed engaging Billy's difference as potential for healthy challenge and opportunity for growth, he viewed engaging my difference as a constant threat. He told me that he feared that I would annihilate him. At some point, I decided that if it was

2. Not his real name.

between him or me, I would choose him. I wanted the relationship to work. And I would do what needed to be done even if it meant losing myself.

His fear of me became resentful hostility which I tried to understand and ameliorate. "More often than not, Liz, I feel an aversion to you." I tried to explain away his upsetting words and behavior to myself. I prayed, believing that God would certainly bring peace and love into our relationship. But the peace did not come—the more I accommodated Billy, the worse he treated me.

At one point, Billy shared one of his beliefs about relationships: "In every relationship, Liz, there's a dominant person . . . and a person who follows . . ." Billy made clear that between the two of us, he expected to be or at least wanted to be dominant. At the time, I disregarded Billy's relational ideal, unaware of just how important it was to him to dominate and control me.

In time, it became clear that we had two relationships—one public, one private. In public, we were an interracial couple that cared about community living and social justice. Those closest to us knew that we had conflict but did not know the extent of it. In private, behind closed doors, Billy was often angry, frustrated, restless, conflicted or confused. He took his negative emotions out on me. He belittled, criticized and shamed me. No one knew about or suspected the emotional violence that was slowly eroding my already attenuated estimation of myself.

I took Billy's abuse because part of me thought I deserved it. I thought he needed me—needed me to help him work through his issues. I thought that his affirmation and approval could somehow make up for the years of rejection I had received as a woman, as a black person. Maybe if I had Billy's love, maybe if I could hold this relationship together, even with all of its problems, then maybe I would be worth something. Maybe others would see that I, too, could be chosen.

I thought that sticking by him, caring for him even while he expressed violence against me, was the womanly, the Christian thing to do. "Dying to myself," meant putting Billy's interests first. If there was a problem with the relationship, I thought it was up to me to fix it. It seems utterly grotesque to me now how my false conceptions about womanhood and Christianity contributed to self destruction.

Among other things, Billy would criticize my appearance. When I resisted his critique, he explained he had every right to demand that his partner look a certain way. He let me know that I could and would need to work out to maintain a weight with which he was comfortable—he did not want a fat wife. He took issue with my clothes; he did not like a sweater of mine so he stole it from my bedroom. He did not like when I wore sweatpants because he said it made me look like the black women in our North Philadelphia community who would walk on the block in their pajamas.

And then there were the comments, "You're not exactly skinny, you know . . . you mean you actually like the way your body is? . . . Yes, I did notice that your arms were getting fat but I didn't want to say anything."

Among other things, I felt alienated by the racial and cultural homogeneity of Billy's circles (where he insisted that we spend much of our time). I was disturbed by the racial animosity that I sensed from him and those who were close to him. In general, it felt as though when there was some racial dissonance or divide, it was up to me to show grace, to be patient, to reach out. As the relationship wore on, I felt greater isolation and disconnection from myself.

Relating to Billy—emotionally, spiritually, sexually—continuously boiled down to which one of us had control or which one of us was dominating the other. In frustration once, I said "I feel like you don't want me to be own separate person." With no sense of irony, Billy agreed with my assessment and said that the more I was like him, the better the relationship would be. I looked at him incredulously—I am black, I am a woman. I cannot be you.

I can remember yelling and fighting back with Billy. I can remember telling him how unfair I thought he was, how upset I was about the double standards that existed in our relationship. When it came to his interests and his work, I was expected to be a supportive and focused girlfriend. When it came to mine, he could be justifiably disengaged. I told him that I felt suffocated, held back by how much time and attention he said he needed from me; I had my own life too. I wanted time to myself. I told him how disrespectful he was to me. I had my voice, it was a weak voice but it was present nonetheless—that was demanding to be heard, to be acknowledged.

Even as I struggled with him, I knew that I would not leave, I was committed to stay. Billy was able to acknowledge that he treated me poorly and that our relationship suffered from intense dysfunction. When he ended our relationship, he said, "I know I need to change but I don't want to." He offered no apologies. And it was over.

I was devastated. I felt that I had tried so hard, had given so much of myself but had failed to keep the relationship together. The grief overwhelmed me. I was in pain I could not understand. It felt like nothing in my faith journey had prepared me for this loss. In my time with Billy, I had been dying slowly, letting parts of myself go and silently wasting away. And now, without the relationship, I despaired because I thought that I had nothing left. I contemplated suicide.

I figured that God was speaking through all of this pain so I let God know that She had my full attention. I began each morning with listening, contemplative prayer. To my surprise, the voice that I heard was my own. The voice that had been silenced, stuffed away, ignored, disrespected, disregarded—was now speaking. I was encountering the voice of resurrection.

Christ, the author of resistance, was inviting me to listen to the voice of resurrection; the voice that affirmed and celebrated my humanity and my belovedness.

As I listened to the voice of resurrection, I was awakened to the presence of death in my relationship with Billy. Billy had done to me what I had learned to do to myself—disrespected me, degraded me, turned his aggression against me. He believed that I was not worth as much as he was, so I deserved to be treated poorly, to be humiliated, to be torn down. There were, arguably, psychological reasons that could explain our interaction—his abusive domination and my submissive co-dependence. But there was also a historical, spiritual reality that was at play.

As I listened to the voice of resurrection, I could admit how I have experienced, practiced, participated in and witnessed manifestations of death: conformity, assimilation, alienation, objectification, American imperialism and militarism, racism, sexism, patriarchy, heterosexism, abuse. And far more tragically than I, so have Trayvon Martin, Rekia Boyd, Matthew Shepard, the people of Haiti, Iraq, Vietnam . . .

As I listened to the voice of resurrection, I could acknowledge that I exist within structures that were not made for me to thrive, to succeed, to flourish. In fact these structures are dependent upon my silence, my destruction. Those who dominate depend on the ones they are stepping on to affirm, legitimate their power; depend on them for survival, for purpose. It will go well with me if I participate, cooperate, accept their legitimacy. If I question or resist, I will be discredited, labeled a conspiracy theorist, marginalized, alienated.

In this season of listening, I found the courage to examine the truth about the "isms"—racism, sexism, capitalism, militarism, male chauvinism, etc. are all power structures which assume scarcity (of love, power, recognition, land, resources, money). The supposed scarcity is used to justify all kinds of violence, murder, exclusion, domination. These power structures present a direct contrast to the fullness of the kingdom of God, where there is enough for everyone and all can live humanly.

As I listened, I could no longer run away from what it meant for me as a woman to have been raised and been part of church communities defined and characterized by male domination. In many of the church communities where I had joined, women were certainly present but their voices were not as important and could not be heard over the men. Women were expected to be supportive "help-meets" that helped their husbands fulfill their divine callings. No one seemed to ask or wonder whether women could have a divine destiny apart from their husbands. There was no room in this reality for single heterosexual women, queer women, women who did not, could not or chose not to have children. In the patriarchal structures I encountered, a woman's value is based on what she brings to a man. I did not come away from these patriarchal church communities unscathed—the lies about a woman's worth that I had swallowed damaged my sense of self. I was in need of much healing.

As I left the Christian community that I shared with Billy, I was being welcomed and folded into another—the Word and World community.[3] In that circle, I found people that gave me the freedom and space to express my black, feminine anger. It was through Word and World that I was introduced to Audre Lorde and William Stringfellow, two activists and authors, who affirmed and gave language to my experience as a black woman.

Lorde, a black, lesbian, warrior poet, spoke powerfully to me. Her essays exposed heterosexism, racism, sexism, classism with such clarity that their weighty implications for my external and internal worlds could no longer be avoided. She told me that I could be loved just as I was: black, female and incredibly angry. She redirected me from my path of self-destruction. Audre Lorde saved my life; she gave me new life.

Lorde said what I could not say, with courage and clarity I could not seem to muster, "Of course I am afraid, because the transformation of silence into language and action is an act of self revelation and that always seems fraught with danger."[4] Indeed, I had been afraid to speak about my pain and my reality because I was certain I would be rejected and cast off.

3. Online: www.wordandworld.org

4. Lorde, "Transformation," 42.

In *An Ethic for Christians*, Stringfellow, an Anglican attorney and lay theologian, describes how all of creation after the fall is subject to the power of death. No one can escape death's reign—no power, principality, institution, government, church, family, corporation. Stringfellow encouraged me—"in the midst of babel, speak the truth."[5] "In the face of death, live humanly."[6] Our resistance to death, as we esteem our humanity and the Word of God, is the way to live humanly.[7] And as we cope with death, we encounter godly hope.

As I read Lorde and Stringfellow in tandem, the ubiquity of death and the absolute need for resistance to its power, particularly for black women, became more apparent to me. We (black women) were born into second (third, fourth) class citizenship. We languish at the very bottom of the American hierarchy. As an attorney, I learned the harsh reality of this hierarchy within my profession. It was clear to me early on that it did not matter how hard I worked, how intelligent I was—I would never be valued as much as a white man. I have had my intellectual capacity/capability challenged and questioned. On more than one occasion, I have had my professional contribution attributed to a white male counterpart.

I live in an America that tells me that I do not belong. White men are inherently valuable—they do not need to prove themselves. They are the rightful heirs of privilege and power. I, however, am illegitimate. I am not entitled to the same power, respect, deference, trust that my white male counterparts are entitled to. The white male voice is normative, objective, superior, trustworthy. I felt a burden, a responsibility to prove America wrong. This enormous weight was lifted from me when I read, "No woman is responsible for altering the psyche of her oppressor."[8] Thank you, Lorde!

For years, I have engaged in an internal negotiation where I must decide how much of myself I will cut off, leave behind, obliterate, kill so that majority folks will not remember my blackness and all the fear that that can hold for them; I lop parts of myself off to make sure not to trigger any of the stereotypes that would normally have them discredit or disregard those who look like me. To my shame, I have differentiated myself

5. William Stringfellow, *An Ethic For Christians*, William Stringfellow Library (Eugene, OR: Wipf & Stock, 2004), 141.

6. Ibid., 142.

7. Ibid., 126.

8. Audre Lorde, "The Uses of Anger: Women Responding to Racism" in *Sister Outsider*, 133 [124–33].

from "other women" or "other black folks" in conversations to let the white hearers/listeners know—"Oh yes, I am on your side. I understand you. I am for you. You don't need to be concerned about me—I'm one of the 'good ones.' I will not burden you with having to see or consider me. No, you don't have to apologize for your ignorance, your offensiveness, your insensitivity. I forgive you." And my reward for social suicide and self-mutilation would be the acceptance and approval of majority culture.

As I continued to delve into listening/contemplative prayer and reflect on Lorde and Stringfellow's words, a remarkable thing happened: I became less afraid to speak my truth. Rather than being silent or internalizing or laughing off situations where my blackness or femininity were denigrated, I began to address them as they were happening. I was less afraid to express my anger over the chauvinism, patriarchy and misogyny within communities that embraced white male domination.

For so long, I had been afraid of who I would alienate with my anger, who would be uncomfortable. I was also afraid of losing hard-won social capital as a "black-woman-you-did-not-have-to-fear-because-she-was-nice-and-would-not-bring-up-anything-to-uncover-your-white-guilt." I believe there are other black women who have done a similar calculus—don't rock the boat, trouble the waters by pointing out the systemic injustice and you can climb that ladder of success if you remain silent. "But at what cost?!" said the voice I was starting to listen to. How much more of myself would I silence to maintain a status quo that in reality did not exist to benefit me anyway? The truth was that all I really needed to be afraid of was losing a false self, a self that could not live into the fullness of who God created me to be.

The relationship with Billy was characterized by death. A great freedom has come to me in recognizing that the things Billy did and said to me were his shame. Not mine. His decision to abuse me was not my fault. Likewise, the things that American society and institutions have done to degrade and undermine my humanity are not my shame to bear.

I am committed to reminding myself each day of my worth and value as a creation of the Most High. I am committed to resisting the power of death and its messengers. I am committed to speaking my truth. I try now to surround myself with and seek community that will recognize and affirm my value. I am determined to decolonize my mind knowing that Carter G. Woodson's words are true: "When you control a man's thinking you do not have to worry about his action . . . You do not need to send him to the back door. He will go without being told. In fact, if there is no back door, he will cut one."[9] I no longer want to be complicit in my annihilation or anyone else's. I want to live humanly.

The work of resistance is a sacred, daily commitment to affirm my humanity in opposition to those who would stamp it out. "Caring for myself is not self-indulgence, it is self preservation (and that is an act of political warfare)."[10] Amen, Audre. Amen.

9. Carter G. Woodson, "Preface," in *The Mis-Education of the Negro* (Washington, DC: Associated Publishers, 1933); online: www.historyisaweapon.com/defcon1/misedne.html

10. Audre Lorde, "Epilogue," in *A Burst of Light: Essays by Audre Lorde* (Ithica, NY: Firebrand, 1988), 131 [131–34].

الرحيم الرحمن الله بسم

In the name of God, Most Gracious, Most Merciful.

16

Hornets at the Roundtable

Life and Death in the Interstitial Margins

EDA RUHIYE UCA

CONTEXT AND COMMITMENTS

> Every form of sharply bounded identity, every absolute of re-
> ligion or roots or story or tradition or gender or sex or race or
> ethnicity or class, already appears to us simplistic, brittle, and a
> bit desperate in its fabrication.[1]

A TIP FROM ONE erstwhile peddler at the sample sale market of subaltern locations: Do not be bamboozled by neatly ordered displays of bias
cut swatches. Look on the backside and you will discover the secrets of
their fabrication.

*I am a North American, Middle Eastern, third wave feminist woman
of color, and Muslim convert to Christianity.*

A pattern for constructing one's hybrid integration in the context of
mutual alienation: *Get a seam ripper and some thread—you'll need them!*

1. Catherine Keller, *God and Power: Counter-Apocalyptic Journeys* (Minneapolis:
Fortress, 2005), 136.

Write a poem in the language that you spoke with unencumbered fluency when you were ten years old. Find cousins on facebook and "like" everything on their walls. Especially pictures of family holidays. Start sentences with, "As a woman of color," out of the earshot of relatives who would correct you, "But we're white! You're white! I'M WHITE!" Go to a dinner party where well-meaning (*really* well-meaning) strangers (*vallahi billahi* they mean well, ya) make a spectacle of you. (*Ama yemin ediyorym ki bunu iyi niyetle yapiyorlar!*) *Yes, I converted from Islam to Christianity. How did my parents react? Was my life ever in danger? Yeah, they killed me. Hang on my mom's on the phone.* Then go home and hem false appropriation and over-simplification and grief and contrived grief and, like maybe, whatever you last read for your feminist theory class. If when you finish, you discover neither/nor holes, just stick on some of those stiff both/and patches you're hiding with the cigarettes in the zippered compartments of your purse.

I am a North American, Middle Eastern, third wave feminist woman of color, and Muslim convert to Christianity.

I really am, sort of. The practice of claiming one's self (even among limited choices) is not without merit and among friends, it is good-enough shorthand for what was said the last time you talked for three hours on the phone, lavishly deconstructing the racist undertones of other people's movement work. And we're friends now, reader; I have told you where I hide my things! (Seriously though: Do not tell my dad that I'm smoking again. I feel guilty enough that I'm still on his wireless plan.)

I am a North American, Middle Eastern, third wave feminist woman of color, and Muslim convert to Christianity. My story is no seamless garment. The seams of my story bind and rend as the meaning of the threads keep shifting. At the unbound edges of my story I discover exotic new threads: American Indian threads, Euro-American feminist threads, African American, African and Latin American liberation, womanist, mujerista, feminist, and post-colonial threads, Southeast Asian and Asian liberative, post-colonial, queer, and feminist threads, and post-structuralist threads. I pull them out of their narrative contexts for possible appropriation.

I fashion the threads into loops to hold keys, braids to fly kites, lines to catch fish, bows to shoot arrows, and slingshots to fling stones. I tie them to my wrists, my ankles, and my hair. I forget them in my purse and they become tangled in impossible knots. I curse these complications. In an effort to order the threads, I weave them into a tablecloth for a roundtable that belongs to no one in particular. I am a poor weaver (I prefer gathering metaphors from the "glossary of sewing terms" entry on Wikipedia to actual weaving) and the tablecloth is an uneven construction. It is fine and lovely, tangled and ugly, coarse and unyielding. The project is unfinished but famished by the effort, I invite my neighbors to the roundtable (Welcome! *Hoş geldiniz! Buyrun!*). I accept their invitation to stay (Why how gracious! *Hoş bulduk!*).

The margins of the roundtable are not *outlier* spaces for mission but *interstitial* (or in between) spaces for meeting. We practice feeding one another in an incomplete mission of mutual liberation. We busy ourselves with the important business of reading fortunes in the inky residue of our coffee cups. We don't notice the tablecloth stretching to fit the margins of a greater table.

While stuffing baklava into our willing mouths some of us become aware of an unwelcome guest at the roundtable: a swarm of hornets. Some friends look away, testifying still of what came before the hornets. Some welcome them as honored guests, recalling heroic hornets past. A wise few begin crushing garlic for salve. (It is known that garlic mixed with water can kill a hornet but one dead hornet is mourned with a hundred stings; they agreed to heal the stings without harming the stingers.) Those who leave the party needed not to look back to know—there was onion on their plates where there was once the sweetest honey.[2]

WE ARE ALL ISRAELITES:
COLONIZATION AND CO-OPTATION IN THE MARGINS

Few biblical motifs are so woven into competing political discourses as the Exodus-Eisodus (entrance) narrative of the Hebrew Bible. The story in short: The war God (Yahweh) of an enslaved people (the Israelites) rises against their fascist worldly leader (Pharaoh), using biological weapons to destroy the land and systematically kill civilians (among them the poorest of the poor (Exod 11:5; 12:29)) in order that His people are free to His—and not the Pharaoh's—service. The people narrowly escape into the wilderness where they become cranky about the accommodations.

2. I am indebted in the writing of this article to all of my teachers and especially the Rev. Dr. Christopher Duraisingh at The Episcopal Divinity School in Cambridge, Massachusetts, and everyone at Sabeel Ecumenical Liberation Theology Center in East Jerusalem with particular thanks to founder and director, the Reverend Dr. Naim Ateek and founding member and executive committee member Cedar Duaybis.

Eventually their war God leads them to a land flowing with milk and honey and indigenous people, Canaanites and others, and "soon [to] flow with blood."[3] He gives His people laws that they may *occupy* the land (Deut 4:1, 25, 6:1, 7:1, 8:1, 9:4–6, 11:8, 10–11, 29, 31). The (indigenous) peoples of the land do not know Him. He is not much of a pluralist; the indigenous peoples must be destroyed. He commands, "you must not let anything that breathes remain alive" (Deut 20:16, Josh 10:40); many of the peoples of the land are slaughtered under the war God's divine mandate in a genocidal campaign which spared not men and women, young and old, oxen, sheep, and donkeys, from the edge of the sword, (Josh 6:21). Again, biological weapons are used; this time *swarms of killer hornets* are applied to drive out or to seek and kill most of those left hiding. The use of the hornets is breathtakingly systematic and effective, to the point of preserving optimal use of the land by the Israelites (Deut 7:22). The natives, too, become weaponized; the war God permits that some survive on the land, in order that He might let them rise against His people when he is displeased with them. Free to serve Him or die, the Israelites emerge as the war bounty of a greater Master than Pharaoh. The tangled threads of oppressed-oppressor-oppressed ensnare (all) the people further, as the Israelites take the people of the land for slaves (Josh 9:21–27; Judg 1:28–35).

A story of divine rage, graphic violence, and rapacious immorality visited on indigenous peoples has all the elements for European and Euro-American colonial and neo-colonial appropriation.[4] Through it, European and Euro-Americans "Israelites" have found just clause to terrorize, enslave, displace, and slaughter "Canaanites" in their own times. In turn, some clever, faithful, and steadfast "Canaanites" (those in the Latin American and African American liberation traditions) flipped the script, naming the European and Euro-American powers and principalities as the Pharaoh, claiming *themselves* to be the Israelites and claiming *for themselves* a God who acts *in* the world against the powers and principalities *of* the world. Ultimately however no transactional change (a mixing up of players) will achieve transformational change (a mixing up

3. Michael Prior, "A Moral Reading of the Bible in Jerusalem," in *Jerusalem in Ancient History and Tradition*, ed. Thomas L. Thompson, Journal for the Study of the Old Testament Supplement Series 381; Copenhagen International Seminar 13 (London: T. & T. Clark, 2003), 28.

4. Michael Prior, *The Bible and Colonialism: A Moral Critique*, Biblical Seminar 48 (Sheffield: Sheffield Academic, 1997), 282–83.

of the game); no exegetical game of musical chairs swapping "bad 'Israel-ites'" (such as white colonizers) for "good 'Israelites'" (such as liberation theologians) will fundamentally redeem the structural injustice underly-ing the premise of the story.

It is important to distinguish some ways such appropriations of the Exodus-Eisodus text have differed: white Pharaoh-Israelites have found a God of conquest; black and brown Canaanite-Israelites have found a God of mercy and justice. White Pharaoh-Israelites have found sym-metry between the entire text and their historical narrative and mythos which testify to escape from oppression and entry and conquest of new land. Black and brown Canaanite-Israelites, more strongly prioritize the Exodus, for many are still teetering—in fact and in narrative resonance—on the edge of the "promised land." In these interstices of fulfillment and hope, where God's conspiratorial release from Pharaoh has come and is still yet to come, there has been no entry into the land of milk and honey and no interaction with the Canaanites.

Thus, when hornets visit the roundtable, the narrative threads of various host-guests remain split not only in *experience* but also in *time*. While some *seem* to look away, preferring to discuss what came *before*, perhaps it is more correct to say that they cannot sense the hornets' pres-ence at all. For them, the Eisodus remains in a narrative future and its symbols of terror remain unread or even, unwritten. The time of Eisodus is for others in the narrative past and present; occupiers cheer the sign of hornets while the occupied organize against them.

But the roundtable offers another way. A roundtable exegesis un-dergirded by a commitment to building missions of mutual liberation invites the experiences and times of oppressed(-and-oppressor) peoples to interrogate the text in dialogue. This polyphonic reading takes seri-ously the many voiced political, theological and cultural narratives in the text and at the table. Such a process will readily reveal that the uncritical appropriation of the Israelite narrative is incompatible with the commit-ment to building missions of mutual liberation. For it will finally speak into Israelite narratives the testimonies of those who read the Bible *not* as Israelites but as "the forgotten ones in the victory, the Canaanites and others, who are pushed aside and exterminated by the religious zeal of the invading Israelites with God on their side."[5] Thus, at the roundtable, narrative threads are not merely ties to one's past but live cords, carrying

5. Ibid., 280–81.

call-and-response nourishment; allowing the productive movement of what is digested, depleted, and dead; and acting upon and being acted upon by all who invite living connection.

THIS LATE IN THE PARTY,
ALL WE HAVE TO DRINK
IS NEW WINE IN OLD WINESKINS
AND OLD WINE IN NEW WINESKINS:
ISRAELITES AND CANAANITES
(THEN AND NOW)

In a roundtable exegesis of the Exodus-Eisodus text, the Palestinian narrative thread is vital indeed. For in Israel-Palestine, the promise of God's exclusive care and justice for the Israelites has played out with a uniquely literalistic ferocity. Zionist political and theological narratives seeking to defend, excuse, obscure, and ignore the military occupation and apartheid system (or *hafrada* and/or *nishool*[6]) in Israel-Palestine conflate the Israelites of the Old Testament with the State of Israel. This, writes the Rev. Dr. Naim Ateek, the father of Palestinian Liberation Theology (PLT), makes the Palestinians appear to represent the old Canaanites who at God's command needed to be dispossessed; the Bible thus becomes a powerful weapon in the hands of a few staunch militants who are ready to act at the behest of their God to repress, kill, and murder their antagonists.[7]

6. *Hafrada* is a Hebrew word meaning "separation," used by Israelis about the government of Israel's policies of separation, such as in *Geder Ha'hafrada* ("separation fence"). The term has been appropriated by some Palestinians and allies as equivalent to the South African *apartheid* ("separation" in Afrikaans). Some Palestinians and allies prefer *nishool*, the Hebrew word for "dispossession." Others use both terms, because each denotes a different aspect of the occupation. For more see Naim Ateek, "The Apartheid Paradigm," *Cornerstone* (Spring 2008) 1–4.

7. Naim Stifan Ateek, *Justice, and Only Justice: A Palestinian Theology of Liberation* (Maryknoll, NY: Orbis, 1989), 84, 86–87. Jewish religious Zionism followed well after American and European Christian Zionism. The first secular Zionists of Jewish heritage were overwhelmingly at odds with religious Jews who railed against the Zionist project for displacing the agency of Messianic promise in God's time with political agency driven by military prowess in man's time. For more see Yakov M. Rabkin, *A Threat from Within: A Century of Jewish Opposition to Zionism*, trans. Fred A. Reed (London: Zed, 2006). Euro-American and European Christians, experienced in linking theologies of supremacy with the colonial enterprise, had no such conflict. Thus Palestinian Christians were made refugees in the name of their own God with the use of their own sacred Scripture and by those in the same one body of Christ. Cedar

Despite the dangers of conflating Canaan then to Canaan now, the narratives of those under occupation (then and now), echo eerily from ancient scripture to modern day seizure and settlements. For who can read the war God's boasting with Palestinian Christian eyes and not also see the *catastrophe* of nearly 800,000 Palestinian refugees from 531 villages emptied by the Nakba of 1948?[8] Who can read it and not rage against the 700km Apartheid Wall, the seizure of hundreds of thousands of *dunums* of Palestinian land, the demolition of some 18,000 homes since 1967, and over 200 illegal settlements (housing some 500,000 Israeli Jews) which continue to displace Palestinians? We have few details of what the Canaanites suffered that the Israelites might live in their towns and eat their fruit, but here are the headlines from the taking of Canaan today: demolition orders are given for tents and rainwater cisterns; thirsty children in refugee camps listen longingly to the splashing of pool water in nearby settlements; urine and garbage are rained on shopkeepers for their steadfast refusal to forfeit their fathers' or grandfathers' storefronts to the settlers above; unable to provide for their families in the economic chokehold of the occupation many become day laborers and build Jewish settlements which they are barred from even visiting; indigenous civilians (including children) are killed in high numbers by the occupying military; no military retaliation on the part of the indigenous population can stand against the vastly superior military power of the occupiers.[9] The cost of an unspeakable crime against a brutally oppressed people (the enslavement of the Israelites and, the unfathomably catastrophic *Shoah* of European Jews) is paid exponentially more so by the indigenous peoples of the land of Canaan than by the perpetrators of the first evil. A live connection to the Palestinian narrative thread forces us to digest the fullness of the war God Yahweh's blessing:

> I have given you a land for which you did not labor and towns
> which you did not build, and you have settled in them; you are

Duaybis, "Palestinian Liberation Theology," (presentation at the 7th annual Sabeel International Young Adult Conference, East Jerusalem, Palestine, July 4–15, 2012).

8. Ilan Pappé, *The Ethnic Cleansing of Palestine* (Oxford: Oneworld, 2006), xiii.

9. For more see Physicians for Human Rights—Israel, "Occupation and Settlements as the Main Determinant of Health for Palestinians in H2-Area in Hebron," (Tel Aviv: Physicians for Human Rights, 2010); Foundation for Middle East Peace, "Israeli Settlements—an Obstacle to a Two-State Peace 1947–2012," (Washington DC: Foundation for Middle East Peace, 2012); United Nations Office for the Coordination of Humanitarian Affairs occupied Palestinian territory, "The Humanitarian Impact of Israeli Settlement Policies" (East Jerusalem: UNOCHA, 2012); PIJ Policy Paper, "Israeli Settlements and the Two-State Solution" (Jerusalem: Palestine-Israel Journal, 2009).

enjoying vineyards and olive groves which you did not plant. (Josh 24:13)[10]

KEEPING THE STORY, SAVING THE PEOPLE: PALESTINIAN LIBERATION THEOLOGY AND THE CONQUEST OF CANAAN

Can the Palestinian Christian escape the hornets—that is, the (apparent) divine terror and death visited on a subaltern people outside of God's covenant—without leaving the Bible behind in the towns they built and the vineyards and groves they planted? Does the Bible offer liberative hope to the Palestinian Christian living under the powers and principalities of occupation? Moreover, is it possible to find such hope without flipping the script of the *Nakba* and occupation, identifying as the true Israelites, and starting anew the cycle of liberation for "God's people" at the expense of others' safety, wholeness, and freedom? Palestinian Christian Liberation Theology (PLT) addresses these questions. Through this hermeneutical lens, Palestinians (and all who are committed to building missions of mutual liberation) are able to keep the story *and* break the devastating cycle wrought by presuming God's exclusive covenantal care.

For Palestinian Christians, the only liberative hermeneutic capable of redeeming the nature and character of God in the Bible and in history and recovering of all of the Bible as "useful for teaching, for reproof, for correction, and for training in righteousness" (2 Tim 3:16) is according to Ateek, "nothing less than Jesus Christ himself [and his teaching]."

> [T]he *Word* of God incarnate in Jesus the Christ interprets for us the *word* of God in the Bible. To understand God, therefore, the Palestinian Christian, like every other Christian, begins with Christ and goes backward to the Old Testament and forward to the New Testament and beyond them.[11]
>
> [Such a hermeneutical key is liberating] for in Christ and through Christ and because of Christ, Christians have been given a revealed insight into God's nature and character . . . [as] a God of love, justice, and peace.[12]

---

10. Reprinted from the *Tanakh: The Holy Scriptures* (Philadelphia: Jewish Publication Society, 1985).

11. Ateek, *Justice, and Only Justice,* 80.

12. Ibid., 79–80, 84.

> [Thus] when confronted with a difficult passage in the Bible [such as those of the Exodus-Eisodus narrative] or with a perplexing contemporary event one needs to ask such simple questions as: . . . Does this fit the picture I have of God that Jesus has revealed to me? . . . If it does, then that passage is valid and authoritative. If not, then I cannot accept its validity and authority.[13]

How then is the Bible recovered if every passage does not agree with the revelation of God in Jesus Christ? Such passages retain their pedagogical value (for teaching, reproof, correction and training in righteousness) in as far as they offer vital insight into a period of human understanding and a dynamic counterpoint to the nature and character of God as revealed in Jesus Christ.[14]

To begin to unpack the PLT hermeneutical method, it is important first to note that while being a foundational testimony to both Judaism and Christianity, "the Old Testament does not stand on its own" in either tradition. Just as the hermeneutical key of Jesus Christ may interpret the Old Testament for Christians, the Mishna and the Talmud of Rabbinic Judaism serve to interpret the Old Testament for Jews.[15]

When read through the hermeneutical key of Jesus Christ, very many passages in the Old Testament *do prove* valid and authoritative. This should come of no surprise. After all, many of the first followers of Jesus found rich resonance between the Jewish scriptures and the life and teaching of Jesus Christ such that they discerned him to be the fulfillment of the hope of those scriptures.[16] However, while Christians find the fulfillment of God's inclusive and universal care for all people in Jesus Christ, both Testaments wrestle with the question of inclusion[17] and grow toward understanding and witnessing to an "inclusive and loving God . . . who reigns over all."[18] Therefore while PLT remains authentic to its own Christian tradition, it also affirms that one need not be a Christian in order to discover God's inclusive and universal vision for humanity. As justice is foundational to all faiths,[19] the sacred scriptures of all faiths offer

13. Ibid., 81–82.

14. Ibid., 79, 83.

15. Naim Stifan Ateek, *A Palestinian Christian Cry for Reconciliation* (Maryknoll, NY: Orbis, 2008), 54.

16. Ibid., 54.

17. Ibid., 54–56, 62–64, 71–75.

18. Ibid., 75, 78, 141, 163.

19. Ibid., 16.

direction and hope to those seeking the way of love, mercy, and peace in their own traditions.

Moreover, in PLT the New Testament and Christian theologies are also "continuously submitted to [the] authoritative concept . . . [of] the revelation of God in Christ."[20] PLT is critical of New Testament passages and Christian theologies entrenched in the systems of oppression which Jesus Christ challenged. Such passages and theologies *are not* valid and authoritative simply because they spring from the Christian tradition.

Therefore PLT does not endeavor to replace Jewish texts, interpretive methods, and theologies with Christian ones but rather to challenge any texts, interpretive methods, and theologies which contradict the hermeneutical key of love, justice, peace, and inclusiveness as is fundamental to all faiths, as is witnessed to in both Judaism and Christianity, and most importantly for Christians, as is characteristic of the life and teachings of Jesus Christ.[21]

Holding onto the Palestinian Liberation Theology thread (clinking with keys from before the catastrophe and after), we can return profitably to the issue of hornets: the war God of the Israelites systematically applied hornets to seek out, purge, and kill defenseless Canaanites because they did not know and serve Him. Does this fit into the picture we have of God revealed in Jesus Christ? In fact, Jesus was turned away from a Samaritan village, populated by those who did not recognize him or share the religion of his traveling companions. His friends asked, *Lord, do you want us to command fire to come down from heaven and consume them?* Jesus rebuked his friends and they left the Samaritans to live in peace (Luke 9:51–62). This event in the life of Jesus is not in the least anomalous to his character. In fact, Jesus *never* coerced others into relationship with him nor permitted the use of violence against those "outside" of his band of followers, whatever such person's past or future faithfulness, nation or race, tradition or culture.

This gives Christians some important clues for considering God's apparent use of hornets in the Exodus-Eisodus narrative. Such a text cannot be a valid and authoritative because it stands in radical opposition to the revelation of God in the life and teachings of Jesus Christ. Thus the PLT hermeneutical key frees everyone at the roundtable from the heavy

---

20. Ateek, *Justice, and Only Justice*, 83.

21. I summarized here some of Ateek's writing on revelation and biblical authority. However, his forthcoming publications give a fuller sense of how he has continued to refine his hermeneutical methodology and the insights proceeding.

yoke and edicts of "a nationalistic god who is more concerned with land than with human beings, with war than with peace."[22]

To this point I have described how PLT comes to an understanding of the nature and character of God. However Christians come to know the revelation of Jesus Christ through the embodied story of one who is both divine *and human*. Just as the revelation of God in scripture and theology is *continuously submitted to the authoritative concept of the revelation of God in Christ*, so too are the aims and means of the Palestinian resistance continuously submitted to the revelation of right relationship in Christ. For, as Ateek writes,

> Like many Palestinian Christians today, Jesus was born under occupation and throughout his life knew only a life under occupation. All his travels, his eating and drinking, his teaching and healing ministry, his relationships with others—every aspect of his life—were carried out under the oppressive domination of the Romans. Finally, he was executed by the occupation forces in collusion with the religious leaders of first-century Jerusalem.[23]

In Jesus, Palestinian Christians find a brother who lived and suffered as they have lived and suffered. As a person living under occupation, Jesus is an exemplar of self-sacrificial friendship, forbearance, mercy, justice, and love. Jesus "counseled the people to resist the occupation by maintaining their human dignity and by taking the initiative by nonviolent means."[24] For PLT, this counsel becomes the rubric against which to measure Palestinian resistance to the occupation.

A FRIEND AT THE TABLE

Jean Zaru, a Quaker feminist Palestinian liberation theologian and Clerk of the Friends Meeting House in Ramallah, makes several contextually informed moves in deconstructing the dominant Exodus-Eisodus narrative. As a Quaker, she is informed by an experience of the inner light, or that which is of God, in every person; she discerns testimonies of *chosenness* through a hermeneutical lens of suspicion. As a Palestinian woman, she has experienced what Asian postcolonial feminist theologian Kwok Pui Lan names as the multiple kyriarchies (or interlocking

22. Ateek, *Justice, and Only Justice*, 85.

23. Ibid., 11.

24. Ateek, *A Palestinian Christian Cry*, 136–37.

layers of oppressions) faced by those in colonized lands.[25] For Zaru, prioritizing *either* national *or* women's liberation is an academic excise and tool of political expediency; she encourages her people to work for the uplift of Palestinian women *and* men, without privileging a masculine/desexed "liberation." Palestinian liberation of any kind will only be achieved through the mutual support of Palestinian women and men, as "two wings of one dove." Thus while the Exodus-Eisodus narrative models seeking justice for one's own group without concern for what would make for justice for others she declares, "it is not enough to take power for myself, my group, my nation . . . I can never accept my liberation at the expense of others . . . liberation is never a transfer of power. It is always a transformation of society."[26]

PLT (in all its iterations) points to the necessity (and eventuality) of an end to the cycle of "redemptive" violence wrought in the name of liberation. At the roundtable, it becomes possible to build missions of mutual liberation undergirded by a commitment never again to mistake a transfer of power with a transformation of power, nor celebrate the liberation of one group at the expense of another.[27]

WHAT CAN WE MAKE OF SUCH A MAKER?
BEASTLY BRETHREN AND BROKEN BODIES
AT THE ROUNDTABLE OF CREATION

> So God created the great sea monsters and every living creature that moves, of every kind, with which the waters swarm, and every winged bird of every kind. And God saw that it was good. (Gen 1:21)

25. Kwok Pui Lan, *Postcolonial Imagination & Feminist Theology* (Louisville: Westminster John Knox, 2004), 55.

26. Jean Zaru, "A Female Palestinian Christian Leader's Voice," presentation at the 7th annual Sabeel International Young Adult Conference, East Jerusalem, Palestine, July 4–15, 2012.

27. Palestinian Christians are not the only "Canaanites" to have wrestled with these questions. George (Tink) Tinker (Wazhazhe Udsethe, Osage Nation) and William Baldridge (Cherokee) describe the problem of the Exodus conquest narrative for American Indians. They call for Indian Christians to transform White Christianity in North America through the retention and aplication of indigenous religious values and traditions. George (Tink) Tinker, "American Indian Theology," in *Liberation Theologies in the United States: An Introduction*, ed. Anthony B. Pinn and Stacey M. Floyd-Thomas (New York: New York University Press, 2010), 171–72.

The hornets remain. The hermeneutical key of Jesus Christ frees those of us at the roundtable from bondage to a God who would weaponize creation and apply it in occupation and war. Nonetheless, the hornets—and the multifarious beasts of terror—remain. If we do not understand God as directing our beastly brethren against us in war, do we imagine that God directs them in peace? Does God choose this or that person to sacrifice on the altar of creation? (*Hm . . . the tiger is hungry. Janet, your time has come.*) Does creation possess an agency of its own apart from God's capacity to intervene? Or does God have the agency to prevent our suffering, and simply ignore our pleas? (*Sorry, Janet.*)

Returning to the hermeneutical key of Jesus Christ: Euro-American feminist theologian Carter Heyward, writes, that God incarnate is known in God's real presence in the "physical, tangible, sexual, painful, humorous, terrible" human experience.[28] This is not a manipulative, hierarchical, controlling, and jealous God but rather one who "both moves and is moved, gives birth and is born, gives and receives, needs and is needed . . . 'the changer and the changed.'"[29] Therefore, to participate fully in the roundtable of creation, Jesus embodies a paradoxical bound-and-freed state wherein, Euro-American feminist theologian Beverly Wildung Harrison says, "to be free means possessing the power to imaginatively interact with others, to give and receive, to act upon and to suffer (that is, to be acted upon), to participate with others in co-creating a world."[30]

Just what kind of world is being created? The Genesis narrative of creation suggests something akin to an orderly liturgy. Yet Euro-American biblical scholar Carol Newsom points to the *wildness* of creation revealed in the book of Job. The book of Job opens with a vision of God as a noble patriarch, "benevolent and paternal . . . [justly] intervening directly to vindicate righteous conduct and punish wickedness."[31] In the realm of the Patriarch God, creation is manipulated to reward, test, or punish human beings; initially the book is suggestively supportive of a positive view of the use of hornets by the war God of the Exodus-Eisodus narrative.

---

28. Carter Heyward, *The Redemption of God: A Theology of Mutual Relation* (Washington DC: University Press of America, 1982), 7.

29. Ibid., 9–10.

30. Beverly Wildung Harrison, *Our Right to Choose: Toward a New Ethic of Abortion* (Boston: Beacon, 1983), 100.

31. Carol A. Newsom, "Job," in *The Women's Bible Commentary*, expanded ed., ed. Carol A. Newsom and Sharon H. Ringe (Louisville: Westminster John Knox, 1998), 143.

However a second view of God and creation emerges in chapters 38–41. Here, God reveals God's *delight* in a creation which is wild, frightful, and bloody.[32] God defies Job's anthropocentric view of nature, revealing everything to be made for its own purpose *and* existing in relationship with the rest of creation. Despite the inherent relationality of creation, creation need not achieve peace within itself in order to draw God's delight; the book of Job presents "an unsentimental view of the natural world in which food for the lion's cubs and the eagle's nestlings means the shedding of blood."[33] Further underscoring this new vision of creation is God's ode to the Leviathan in chapter 41; the Leviathan is gloriously made in such a way that it *will* elicit terror in human beings. The imbalance of power between us assures that any effort to tame, contain, or negotiate with the Leviathan will fail.[34]

Therefore, we and that (or those) which terrify and kill us come to the roundtable by the invitation of the same one God who birthed us (all) into existence. This does not imply an internally consistent code of conduct among God's creatures. In our magnificent diversity, while some creatures will necessarily terrify and kill us, human beings express both the capacity to terrorize and kill *and* to negotiate and cooperate in community. Moreover, for Christians, Jesus Christ serves as a model of righteous nonviolence and holy justice meted out with mercy. (Those of other faiths have other good models.) Yet, as one cannot negotiate with hornets and the beasts of terror, the wild metes and margins of being promise neither safety, nor peace, nor happiness.[35]

What can we make of such a maker? Is God a capricious and evil creator for making us without promise of safety, peace, and happiness? Is God the ghastly orchestrator of our experience of terror and killing? Palestinian Liberation Theology would tell us, *No*, for this is inconsistent with the image of God revealed in the life and teachings of Jesus Christ. Is God then a weak or impersonal force in God's own created order? Keller offers another way to understand God: "this epiphany does not deprive God of agency, or reduce [God] to the impersonal force of nature." She quotes Newsom's exegesis of Job:

32. Ibid., 143–44.

33. Ibid., 144.

34. Ibid.

35. This is clearly a deeply anthropomorphic reading of vulnerability at the margins of creation; there is no beast of terror on earth whose sum output has generated more terror and killing against other creatures than the human being.

> This new image is one of God as a power for life, balancing the
> needs of all creatures, not just humans, cherishing freedom, full
> of fierce love and delight for each things without regard for its
> utility, acknowledging the deep interconnectedness of death
> and life, restraining and nurturing each element in the ecology
> of all creation.[36]

Our vulnerability and power in this primal interconnectedness may
bring us into the experience of terror and killing. More still, our vulnerability and power continue even *beyond* death. For this is the shocking
dignity of the human body at the interstitial margins of the roundtable:
whatever the cause of our demise, will be bread and wine for maggots.
We will be fertilizer for dandelions. Randy bees will nestle in the petals
of our memories. They will carry us to their hives and our bodies will
be made honey. The honey will be cultivated and eaten by those on the
northern side of the grave. Should a child return the honey her mother
fed her in order that our bodies re-member their parts? No. We die that
our bodies nourish her body. Our deaths nourish her life. We are all fated
to be a delicious morsel for eating and very fine mulch, broken for us, and
us, and us, forever and ever, amen. Knowing *all* bodies to be fated for this
rite may point us to a deep goodness in the interconnectedness of all our
relations, even in the absence of hope for a mission of mutual liberation
among us (at least in any conventional sense).

Thus while the military terrorism of the God of the Exodus-Eisodus
narrative cannot be accepted as valid and authoritative teaching, God
does indeed create, love, restrain, and nurture a community of creation
in which some will experience terror and killing in the course of each
coming into the fullest expression of its being. The roundtable is much
greater than we once imagined—and its interstitial margins much more
dangerous, indeed.

36. Keller, *God and Power*, 144.

17

Deadly Betrayal . . .
and a Return to Childhood Faith[1]

NELSON JOHNSON

THE FOG HUNG HEAVY over Greensboro, North Carolina, early on the morning of November 3, 1979. As one of the organizers of an anti-Klan march to be followed by a labor conference, I was a little worried about the weather. Around 7 a.m. I stopped by the home of Jim and Signe Waller, a Jewish couple, where we had breakfast together. Jim had left the medical faculty at Duke University to become an organizer in a textile mill. Little did I know that this was the last time that we would ever have a meal together. In less than four hours Jim would be shot in the back.

By 10 a.m. the fog had melted away and the sunshine had burst through, transforming the day into a bright crisp fall morning. I was excited about the plans for the day. Impressive work had been done in the textile mills along a seventy-five mile stretch of the I-85 corridor and in communities in those mill towns. Greensboro was the center of our textile mill and community work. I felt that a lot of people would be joining the march and attending the labor conference. As a student leader at North Carolina Agricultural and Technical State University and a community organizer, I had organized a number of marches and rallies over the past fifteen years. As usual, I was a little anxious before the big march

1. This article first appeared in the *Witness* 84/3 (2001) 27–29 and is reprinted by permission of The Archives of the Episcopal Church.

and conference, but anticipating mill folk and folk from the black community getting together—a meeting long overdue, I felt like a wonderful day was taking shape.

This initial assessment would prove tragically wrong. By the morning of the next day, I wore clothes splattered with day-old dried blood—blood from five of my dear friends killed the day before by Klan and Nazi gunmen in the streets of Greensboro. I had spent a painful night locked up charged with inciting to riot after a paid police agent led a caravan of nine Klan and Nazi members into a legally planned march, where they killed five people, wounded ten others and terrorized Morningside Homes, an African American public housing community.

I had discussed the march with the police, painstakingly obtained a parade permit, and was assured of police presence and protection. I had had a difficult relationship with the Greensboro police since my student days ten years earlier. The discussion with police immediately came to my mind as I peered through unbelieving eyes on that Saturday morning at the wounded and dying bodies of friends. As the blood of my loved ones was soaking into the ground, I stood over Jim's body and shouted with all the assurance that the Spirit could give me, "This could not have happened without direct police involvement and we declare war on you!"

Of course, I did not know of the police agent's organizing role or any of the other information that eventually came out in court after six long years that resulted in two leading police officers and six Klan and Nazi party members being found liable for wrongful death. At the time, I just knew the police were deeply involved in this tragic event, and I spoke the truth as it was flowing through me. I was immediately charged with inciting to riot, wrestled to the ground and taken to jail. I remained in jail that night because the magistrate refused to set a bond as I was declared to be too great a danger to the peace and order of the city to be set free that day.

Released by mid-morning on November 4, I was met by a small crowd of reporters and friends and informed of the names of those killed. They included not only Dr. Jim Waller and Sandy Smith, the beautiful black former Student Government President at Greensboro's all women's Bennett College, but also Michael Nathan, a Jewish doctor who was leading the first aid team for the planned four-mile march, Cesar Cauce, a wonderful brother of Hispanic origin, who organized among non-academic workers at Duke University, and William (Bill) Sampson, a Virginian by birth and the only Anglo-white. Bill had left divinity school at

Harvard University a few years earlier to become a textile mill organizer in Greensboro.

Once out of jail I also gratefully learned that my eight- and nine-year-old daughters had been picked up by my youngest brother and taken to his home in Winston-Salem for safety. My wife, Joyce, and I drove to a friend's house, as it was too dangerous to move back into our home. The next six days, leading up to the funeral of those killed, were the most intense, the most packed with counterintelligence maneuvering and growing tension, ever in my life and, I suspect, ever in the life of this community of 200,000 citizens—North Carolina's third largest city. These six days would portend the next six years, which involved an intense journey of survival for me and other members and friends of the Communist Workers Party (CWP). This journey involved a strange blending of vicious anti-communism and deep-seated racism, threading through three trials (averaging over five months each) related to the Klan/Nazi killings, the bringing of seven criminal charges against me, slander and vilification of those killed and those of us who survived on a scale that I had never seen before. Yet, all of this did not stop a powerfully inspired fight back and for me a rediscovery of my faith on a deeper level.

My faith was nurtured in the late 1940s and early 1950s on a farm near Littleton, in eastern North Carolina. We black folk formed a fairly tight rural community, but we were completely separated from whites except for the requirements of work. Religion was central to our village. My grandfather, for whom I was named and who died in 1932, was the founder and first pastor of Lee's Chapel Baptist Church. My father, now ninety-two years old, was a deacon in the church and my mother, who died at eighty-seven in 1992, played the piano for the church choir. I grew up surrounded by religion and faith. It was so real and so profound for many people in our little village. As a child and teenager, I liked the singing and the preaching (preaching has a very lively form in the southern black rural tradition). However, the deeper substance and interiority of the faith never fully gripped me, although I am convinced that it gripped many other people in the community. I wanted to feel and believe as deeply as they seemed to feel and believe, I just didn't. But even with my shallow awareness, I was a believer, I went along with what I understood the faith to be.

I suppose that part of the basis for my faith is because religion and church were the stabilizing force in the community. In fact, church was the only significant institution in the community other than the school. It served the role of being a community center, recreation center, old folks home, counseling service, arts and drama club, civic center and faith center, all wrapped into one. It was really the unifying epicenter of our village.

As for Jesus, I really didn't think much about who he was in my early years. I certainly didn't have a frame of reference on how or whether the human and divine dimensions came together in Jesus. Such theological reckoning was not even a thought. He was just the Savior, who did miracles, helped people and assured us that everything would be all right. In the midst of this racially oppressed and segregated community, Jesus helped us put up with "white folk" in the hope of going to heaven in another life. My faith did not grow out of well-considered reflection on the meaning of anything in particular. Rather, it was the acceptance— and I did accept it—of the general feeling, mood and beliefs in my small rural community. We believed that there was a God and that God would reward the good people and punish the bad people; Bible stories were told in such a way as to reinforce that. If you asked God, God would have mercy on you, even if you were mean, because he was a forgiving God. Such was my early faith training.

I matured slowly. People my age always seemed more grown-up than I was. Through my four years in the US Air Force and later my growing involvement in the black liberation movement, particularly my study of Marxism, I gently laid aside many of my previous faith beliefs. There was so much about religion that didn't make sense to me in my late twenties and thirties. I gradually moved away from organized religion and dedicated my life to working among the poor. I was committed to doing what I could to help folk, including working with religious people and the church when I thought that would help. Although I did not make a public spectacle of it, I no longer considered myself to be a confessing believer in the former sense.

During the six-year period after November 3, 1979, of being denounced, labeled, branded, stigmatized and ostracized, I was alternately drawn to reflecting more on faith and things of the Spirit and then pushed farther away from religion because I thought the church should have been doing more. In 1983 I believe, I was serving a twenty-day sentence for contempt of court. I had refused to stand when the judge entered the court because the court, in my opinion, was so corrupt. I had seen two all-white juries acquit all the Klan and Nazi gunmen of all criminal charges in spite of the fact that they were filmed by four television stations, calmly shooting people. I had lost all respect for the court.

While serving the twenty days, I went on a twenty-day hunger strike to express further contempt for the court. An Episcopalian minister attached to the University of North Carolina in Greensboro, Henry Atkins, visited me in my jail cell one day and inquired as to my well-being. I didn't know him. He seemed like a very kind man. I sensed in him something very authentic. I asked him what he really believed. "Do you really believe there is a God and, if so, how do you explain the sort of thing that happened here in Greensboro and especially the role of church folks?" Honestly, I cannot remember exactly what Atkins said, but I remember what he didn't say, and I remember how I felt. He didn't give me the expected heavy-handed speech about how God was going to deliver me or punish someone else or the bit about my need to have more faith. As best I can recall, he shared a little about his life and about what God meant to him personally. It didn't sound all that strong at the time, but I felt it was genuine. It was enough for me to begin to wrestle anew with my own faith.

When I got out of jail, Atkins invited me to St. Mary's House, a little church adjacent to the college campus. About twenty-five Christian ministers were there, mostly white. They were courteous but obviously did not understand the depth of the systemic evil and the need for change.

From 1979 through 1984, I felt like I went through hell. I reached the end of my rope. I spent many nights agonizing over what I needed to do in the future. Driven by circumstances and inspired by discussion with Atkins and others, I started to read the Scriptures a little. I went to a number of churches in the black community, trying to draw meaning from what was being preached. A black pastor who was particularly helpful to me was Otis L. Hairston of Shiloh Baptist Church. He was a quiet, unassuming man who preached a gentle gospel that not only invited individual transformation, but also challenged institutional powers and systemic evil. My family and I became members of Shiloh, and it was under Hairston's leadership that I was both protected and initially nurtured in the gospel ministry.

There was a warmth and reception of me in the black church that I had not received anyplace else. What I heard, however, often didn't seem to address the problems of the structured and the systemic evil. What these services did do was to reinvigorate my interest in Jesus. I started to focus on Jesus. As I did, I gradually discovered a person that I hadn't known existed. I was beginning to see how thoroughly Jesus opposed all the sources of evil rooted deeply in culture and manifested through systems. I also sensed a compelling compassion in him for everyone, especially for the poor. I could begin to see how deeply some people loved him and how much others hated him.

Out of the anguish and hardship born from the Klan and Nazi killings on November 3, 1979, I reluctantly returned to the faith of my childhood. Still seeing through a glass darkly, I began to discover in Jesus the kind of deep reliance on God that sustained Him in challenging the powers and principalities and enduring the cross. As I rediscover Jesus on deeper and deeper levels, a new world—the necessity for authentic community lived on the basis of very different assumptions—is opening up to me. It's a challenging but beautiful journey.

18

Cry *¡Presente!* Now and Forever

PABLO RUIZ[1]
TRANSLATED FROM SPANISH BY JULIA MACRAE

I WAS INTRODUCED TO the School of the Americas[2] Watch (SOA Watch) movement about the same time I was introduced to e-mail. It was in early 2000, when I was active in the Kamarikun Human Rights Committee, which operated in a Catholic parish south of Santiago, Chile. I got to know SOA Watch because Eduardo Villaseca,[3] a Chilean living in Minnesota, wrote telling us of the struggle in the United States to close the School of the Americas.

In November of that year I published an interview with grassroots SOA Watch activist Villaseca, called: "School of the Americas: The sword of Damocles over the Latin American peoples." In the first paragraph, written twelve years ago, I said:

> Next weekend in Georgia thousands of human rights activists will gather once again to call for the closing of the sinister School of the Americas. The activities will begin with an all-night vigil on Friday, continue on Saturday with songs, testimonies and speeches, concluding on Sunday, around noon,

---

1. Pablo Ruiz is a Chilean activist and journalist who was arrested, tortured, and imprisoned for two years because of his human rights work late in the Pinochet dictatorship.

2. In 2001, in response to the movement to close it, the SOA was re-named the Western Hemisphere Institute for Security Cooperation or WHINSEC.

3. Eduardo Villaseca died in his apartment in October 2001. *¡Presente!*

with a large number of those present entering Fort Benning, where the "School of Assassins," as many call the military academy, operates.

Who are they? What are the names of these murdered brothers and sisters? What did they look like? How did the people who loved them feel? Why remember them? Why do they cry *¡presente!* at vigils they have been holding for more than twenty years now?

A GROWING MOVEMENT

In the interview, Eduardo Villaseca told me about the origin of SOA Watch and its founder Father Roy Bourgeois. He told me that the movement began in 1990 with a small group who undertook a fast to comemortate the killing of six Jesuits and two women at the University of Central America (UCA) in El Salvador on November 16, 1989. The massacre was ordered and carried out by members of the Atlacatl Battalion, an elite counterinsurgency unit of the Salvadoran Army, created in 1980 at the SOA.[4]

Now there are thousands of activists: men and women, religious, trade unionists, students, veterans for peace, who support the movement calling for the close of the school. Villaseca joined because he had read a short article about Sister Rita Steinhagen, 73, who was in prison for protesting the School of the Americas in the late nineties. "How could I not support her? If Sister Rita was able to go to jail to try to correct the many injustices that she had known in Latin America, I personally had no escape," Villaseca told me.

Steinhagen is one of many SOA Watch former prisoners of conscience. Another former prisoner, Judith Kelly, says she got involved in SOA Watch in 1994 and organized a forty-day vigil and fast on the steps of the United States Capitol. "For me, it was extremely important to support the efforts of SOA Watch. I had gone to El Salvador in April 1994 as an observer of the elections and on that trip I visited the site of the slaughter at the UCA and the chapel where Archbishop Romero was murdered."

In November 1997, on the eighth anniversary of the slaughter of the Jesuits, Father Roy Bourgeois and SOA Watch staff person Carol Richardson welcomed about two thousand protestors to Columbus, Georgia

---

4. Jack Nelson-Pallmeyer, *School of Assassins: Guns, Greed and Globalization*, rev. ed. (Maryknoll, NY: Orbis, 2001), 7.

where Fort Benning is located, no less than five times the number of the previous year. All states except Hawaii were represented. Interrupting the prayers, music and short speeches, police with loudspeakers warned those present that partisan political activity an the base was illegal and that anyone who crossed the line at the entrance would be breaking the law. However, saying there was no higher law than God's, Bourgeois and Richardson ignored the warning and led a solemn funeral procession onto the base. Activists carried coffins and petitions signed by nearly a million people calling for the abolition of the school. Hundreds of people carried white crosses and stars of David, with the names of those killed by graduates of the school. All those names were sung into a microphone, the crowd chanted in unison: *¡presente!* they are present with us.

At that time, Judith Kelly tells me, 601 people crossed the line with Roy and Carol, and of these, 28 had to go to court. The worst thing was that Roy and Carol, the two key leaders of the movement, had to go to prison and Carol's daughter was left to run the Washington DC office.[5]

Theresa Cameranesi, board member of SOA Watch San Francisco, became involved in the movement in the late nineties. She remembers that the year of her first protest at Fort Benning it rained a lot and was cold. Theresa helped as interpreter and facilitator for Salvadoran people who participated in the actions. She was also on the First Aid team, the first year the numbers required one.

Judith Kelly's first vigil was in November 1999. She traveled by bus to Fort Benning with members of Pax Christi.[6] That year was the tenth anniversary of the slaughter at the UCA. Along with others who had experiences in Haiti, she remembers bringing paintings and posters commemorating the first massacre at St. Jean Bosco church in Port-Au-Prince (September 11, 1988). The killing was directed by Franck Romain, a 1959 graduate of the SOA. They also brought a very moving canvas that read: "Remembering the victims of Haiti: the torturer is forgotten, the victim is remembered."

By the end of the decade the vigil was a tradition: on the Sunday morning the names of all those killed or disappeared by graduates of the

5. James Hodge and Linda Cooper, *Disturbing the Peace: The Story of Father Roy Bourgeois and the Movement to Close the School of the Americas* (Maryknoll, NY: Orbis, 2004) 176.

6. Pax Christi is an international Catholic peace movement established after World War II. It works around the world on human rights and disarmament projects and campaigns. Online: www.paxchristi.net

School of the Americas are read aloud. By naming their names, thousands and thousands of people were saying and are saying: ¡presente!

Hendrik Voss who edits the SOA Watch newsletter ¡Presente![7] says that the word *itself* is part of the movement. "The word ¡presente! is used in the ritual at the gates of Fort Benning, Georgia, when we remember those who have suffered and have been martyred by graduates of the School of the Americas. We say their names and evoke their spirits, and their testimonies are before us when we respond, '¡presente! You are here with us, we do not forget and your death was not in vain.'"

The tradition of reading the names of those killed by politically repressive regimes has a long tradition in Latin America. At Pablo Neruda's funeral on September 25, 1973 in Chile, attendees responded with ¡presente! shouting the names of Neruda, the poet, and Salvador Allende, the recently deposed and assassinated president. This was the first public act of protest against the regime of Augusto Pinochet.

Father Roy recalls that the use of the word ¡presente! was a Central American tradition adopted by those who gathered at the gates of Fort Benning at the first fast in 1990. But the mass-movement use of the word ¡presente!, the procession, and the use of crosses with names gradually became established over the years, as the SOA Watch established its identity as a movement.

Judith Kelly remembers her first vigil, attended by thousands. "As I watched the crowd, that Sunday morning, I saw people I had met through years of delegations to Guatemala, El Salvador and Haiti. At that moment I felt an affirmation of my life as a nonviolent activist, a moment of almost divine discovery—looking at so many inspiring people who I had known through my work for peace. At that moment, for me, there was no other place on earth where I could be."

Father Roy asked everyone for a moment of silence before the procession. They all became completely silent. Then, Kelly remembers, a beautiful voice began to chant the names and all responded ¡presente! Kelly was moved to tears to remember all those lives extinguished by the hatred and violence perpetrated by graduates of the School of the Americas all over Latin America.

Theresa Cameranesi recalls a year that thousands of people crossed the white line drawn on the ground, separating Fort Benning from the public road. "Many were dressed in the black of mourning, with their

7. Published three times a year and sent free to 46,982 subscribers.

faces painted. They were activists, clergy, students. Some theater groups helped in the preparations."

Theresa was impressed by the number of children who were named. "It disturbs me, moves me, How could they kill so many children? Were they perhaps enemies? No answer. Nothing can justify so many deaths, torture and disappearances. It's incomprehensible."

"I joined the movement to honor my Paraguayan father. For the people who were tortured. I realize that police received training from the military and the CIA. I felt the constant pain of many people, (among them Martín Almada[8]) who also were humiliated."

Eduardo Villaseca said that going to the vigil at Fort Benning "is an almost indescribable experience. The solidarity of our group is extraordinary. With our demonstrations we hope to give voice to the victims of this genocide that has been perpetrated the length and breadth of our America. The funeral procession in honor of the victims, with which we enter into the interior of the military base, where the school is located, is a spiritual force without precedent. It seems that one can hear the groans of pain of the tortured and the anguished cries of the families of the victims. The spiritual power of this demonstration is so respected by the military forces that they do not dare to intervene."

THE DUTY TO REMEMBER

There are thousands and thousands of people who have been killed and disappeared in the last fifty years throughout Latin America. Behind the vast majority of these deaths are soldiers trained and supported by the successive governments of the United States.

"Behind these names there are thousands of memories, mixed feelings. Of wealth and poverty, absence and presence, of honor and humiliation," Theresa Cameranesi tells me.

"I feel that our country needs to repent of its evil deeds," said Judith Kelly, adding that "thousands of people in Latin America have been negatively affected by political decisions made by US leaders."

---

8. Martín Almada is a Paraguayan lawyer and human rights activist who was imprisoned and tortured and his family members killed in the 1970s. In 1992 Almada found the "Terror Archives," documentation of Latin American military and security force cooperation in a massive international campaign of terrorism and repression in the name of anti-Communism during the 1970s and '80s.

"Through remembering this sad story, full of loss, plainly connected to the international policies of our government, we are inspired to respond with actions of solidarity and justice. We need to know these stories, remember the pain, and recognize our responsibility and complicity. Then we can advocate for better policies and make good decisions on next steps to be taken," Kelly points out.

As a student, Nico Udu-gama, the newest SOA Watch staff-member, organized busses from his university to participate in the actions at Fort Benning. "Then, after working nearly four years in Colombia with communities resisting the war, this path took me to the SOA Watch office, to give more energy to this anti-imperialist struggle."

For Nico the word *¡presente!* represents a challenge. "Our constant presence, our vigil, our actions are like a cry in the darkness, and we refuse to be forgotten. Forgetting has always been the tool of the powerful to keep punishing and plundering the people. Together we never forget. We know that a better world is possible. We will continue the struggle with our truths and our bodies and I know we will win."

Judith Kelly brings pictures every year of those she especially wants to remember and honor. In recent years she held up the photo of Ramon Gonzalez Ortega. Ortega is the father of Carolina Gonzalez Toro whom she met in 2008 while participating in a delegation to Chile. Carolina was only 10 years old on October 11, 1973 when her father was taken. "He was a government employee and not politically active. He was imprisoned on Dawson Island, in an isolated concentration camp in the remote south of the country. They told him he would be released with other prisoners but eventually shot him in the back on October 30, 1973." In March 2012, Judith Kelly traveled to Punta Arenas, Chile, and paid tribute to him and other victims in the region of Magallanes.

"Remember, to say *¡presente!* is not just important for the SOA Watch movement but to the world, to people, to society. This is about morality, ethics; we must not forget so much horror, so many crimes. In the word, *¡presente!* they are still living, their spirits, their souls, their memories, in those they have loved. They will live forever where there is love," says Theresa Cameranesi.

FLOWER IN THE WIND

Fortunately, thousands of women and men are able to remember every day, in Latin America and around the world. They will continue to lift up the photos and names of our dead, who are alive in our cry for justice.

For example, in May 2009, I met Bertha Oliva, coordinator of the Committee of Relatives of the Detained and Disappeared of Honduras. Bertha often throws a flower in the wind for her friend Nativí Thomas, wherever in the world he may be. Thomas was disappeared in 1981. Bertha continues to fight for justice for the disappeared, so that they will not be forgotten.

On our last night in Honduras, at a farewell dinner, I presented Bertha with a book of poems by Pablo Neruda on behalf of SOA Watch. That night in her honor and in honor of our disappeared companions, I read the poem, "Oda al hombre sencillo," by the Chilean Nobel Prize–winning poet.

With my voice almost breaking I read these verses:

> Ven, no sufras,
> ven conmigo,
> porque aunque
> no lo sepas,
> eso yo sí lo sé:
> yo sé hacia dónde vamos,
> y es ésta la palabra:
> no sufras
> porque ganaremos,
> ganaremos nosotros,
> los más sencillos
> ganaremos,
> aunque tú no lo creas,
> ganaremos.[9]

> Come, don't suffer
> come with me
> because although
> you don't know it
> I do.
> I know where we are going
> and this is the word:
> Don't suffer

9. Reprinted with permission of the Pablo Neruda Foundation, administered by Carmen Balcells Literary Agency. English translation by Julia MacRae.

> because we will win
> we will win
> the most humble,
> we will win
> although you don't believe it
> we will win.

I am convinced that we will win because, as Inés Ragni, mother of the Plaza de Mayo, says, "If we don't resist, our children will disappear again."

19

A Peaceful Warrior Lives On in Us[1]

FRIDA BERRIGAN

I die with the conviction, held since 1968 and Catonsville, that nuclear weapons are the scourge of the earth; to mine for them, manufacture them, deploy them, use them, is a curse against God, the human family, and the earth itself.

—PHILIP BERRIGAN

MY DAD DIED NINE years ago this week. Talking about waging nonviolence and little insurrections.

In life, as in dying, my dad was a peaceful warrior.

In the fall of 2002, after months of feeling lousy and only very slowly healing from hip surgery, Phil Berrigan, priest, peace activist, father of the plowshares movement[2] and three kids, went to the doctor. The verdict came back harsh: advanced (Stage IV) and aggressive liver cancer that had metastasized to his kidneys. The doctors said they could treat it with

1. In Zuccotti Park, in the heart of the Occupy Movement, Frida Berrigan delivered this speech on the life and death of her father Philip Berrigan one of the founders of the North American Christian peace movement. It is reprinted with her permission and first appeared Dec. 9, 2011, on the Waging Nonviolence website under a Creative Commons Attribution-Share Alike 3.0 United States License. Online: www.wagingnonviolence.org

2. For more on plowshares see Arthur K. Laffin, and Anne Montgomery, eds., *Swords into Plowshares: Nonviolent Direct Action for Disarmament, Peace and Social Justice*, Catholic Worker Reprint Series (Eugene, OR: Wipf & Stock, 2010).

chemotherapy, but the chances of a full recovery were slight. Dad was up for trying chemo and wanted to give the doctors—oncologists at the top of their game at Johns Hopkins—a chance, but after one round of chemo, he said "no more."

Friends from far and wide offered alternative cures, advice, great stories of teas and herbs that (against all odds) allowed them to live cancer-free. But, our dad sat us down and told us that he was seeking healing, not a cure; putting his faith in God and in us—praying for healing and for the faith to be strong in the months to come and asking us to start preparing for a life without him. He was not afraid, he told us. He loved us and he was sad, but he would be ready.

And then, with clear eyes and a lot of compassion, he got down to the hard work of dying with dignity.

The hallmark of the next few months was gratitude. I would sit and read with him. "Thanks, Freeds," he'd say. My sister would bring him a drink. "Thanks, love," he'd say. My brother would spend time with him. "Thanks for giving an old man a lift," he'd say. My mom, the Jonah House community,[3] the continuous stream of friends and relatives who came to say hello, spend some time, and say goodbye all experienced the same thing—thanksgiving. Dad allowed no gesture, however small, to go unappreciated.

When some of the day-to-day care became too much for us, we brought in hospice care. They were amazing. They respected what we were doing—loving our dad on his journey to death. Letting him die the way he lived; surrounded by people, surrounded by love, resisting the medical-industrial-complex. There must have been twenty-five people staying at our house during those last two week of Dad's life and we all had a role to play. Our sister-in-law Molly and I cut up Dad's clothes and made a banner that said, "They Shall Beat Their Swords into Plowshares. Nations Shall Learn War No More." He had so few clothes that we had to use a pair of drawers for "Nations."

He stopped eating; he did not want to drink. His breath grew labored. Magnified by the baby monitor in his room, his breathing became the off-kilter metronome of our days, as we planned the funeral, shared stories and memories, prayed, cried, and laughed.

On December 6, sometime after dinner, he died. We stood around him and prayed and cried and said goodbye. The pine box that my brother

3. In addition to their nonviolent resistance actions and organizing, the Jonah House community live on the grounds St. Peter's cemetery West Baltimore and tend the gardens and graves. For more on Jonah House, see online: www.jonahhouse.org

and friends made was ready, beautifully painted by iconographer Bill Mc-Nichols.[4] We prepared the body and laid him in the coffin in dry ice.

The wake and funeral were both at Saint Peter Claver, where he had served as a priest decades earlier. The night after the wake, we gathered around him one last night and then nailed the coffin closed. I remember my Uncle Jim—my dad's oldest living brother at the time—driving nails deep with just two whacks at the hammer, in contrast to my own clumsy, off centered pings with the hammer.

The next morning was cold and clear, so beautiful. Dad was loaded on to the back of a pickup truck and my sister Kate, Molly and I rode in the truck with him while most people processed carrying signs and banners to the church for the funeral mass.

I don't remember that much of the service, but it was a strangely happy occasion. Dad was gone, but in a room full of people who loved him, he was still so present. That presence was the theme of Kate and my eulogy. We took turns reading paragraphs, it is nice for me to go back and hear her voice in some of the lines:

> He is still very present to us, and the work we do (all of us), today and tomorrow and for the rest of our lives, will keep our dad close to us.
>
> He is here with us every time a hammer strikes on killing metal, transforming it from a tool of death to a productive, life-giving, life-affirming implement.
>
> He is here with us every time a member of the church communicates the central message of the gospel (thou shalt not kill) and acts to oppose killing, rather than providing the church seal of approval on war.
>
> He is here whenever joy and irreverent laughter and kindness and hard work are present.
>
> He is here every time we reach across color and class lines and embrace each other as brother and sister . . .

I have spent a lot of time thinking back on my dad's life this week, and it makes my heart open wide and smile to know how present he is in the struggle and cacophony, the hard-born miracle that is Occupy . . . Everywhere.

Kate and I ended by saying:

---

4. For more on iconographer Father William Hart McNichols, see William Hart McNichols and Mirabai Starr, *Mother of God: Similar to Fire* (Maryknoll, NY: Orbis, 2010). Online: www.fatherbill.org

Thanks, Dad, for lessons in freedom, inside and outside of prison. And thanks to all of you for struggling toward freedom and working to build a just and peaceful world. Our dad lives on in you.

Thanks to everyone out there doing the hard, life-giving work right now.

Recommended Reading

*A short list of titles recommended
by the editor and contributors*

Berrigan, Daniel. *Sorrow Built a Bridge: Friendship and AIDS*. The Daniel Berrigan Reprint Series. Eugene, OR: Wipf & Stock, 2009.

Brueggemann, Walter. *The Prophetic Imagination*. 2nd ed. Minneapolis: Fortress, 2001.

Callahan, Maggie, and Patricia Kelley. *Final Gifts: Understanding the Special Awareness, Needs and Communications of the Dying*. New York: Bantam, 1992.

Dancing Heart, Maria. *The Last Adventure of Life: Sacred Resources for Living and Dying from a Hospice Counselor*. 2nd rev. and enhanced ed. Findhorn, Scotland: Findhorn Press, 2008.

Groves, Richard F., and Anne Klauser. *The American Book of Living and Dying: Lessons in Healing and Spiritual Pain*. Berkeley: Celestial Arts, 2009.

Harris, Mark. *Grave Matters: A Journey through the Modern Funeral Industry to a Natural Way of Burial*. New York: Scribner, 2007.

Kübler-Ross, Elisabeth. *On Death and Dying: What the Dying Have to Teach Doctors, Nurses, Clergy and Their Own Families*. New York: Touchstone, 1969.

Lorde, Audre. *Sister Outsider: Essays and Speeches*. The Crossing Press Feminist Series. Freedom, CA: Crossing Press, 1984.

Mitford, Jessica. *The American Way of Death Revisited*. New York: Vintage, 2000.

Nouwen, Henri M. J. *Our Greatest Gift: A Meditation on Dying and Caring*. San Francisco: HarperSanFrancisco, 1994.

Saunders, Cicely. *Cicely Saunders: Selected Writings 1958–2004*. New York: Oxford University Press, 2006.

Smith, Suzanne E. *To Serve the Living: Funeral Directors and the African American Way of Death*. Cambridge, MA: Belknap, 2010.

Stringfellow, William. *An Ethic for Christians and Other Aliens in a Strange Land*. 1973. Reprinted, The Stringfellow Library. Eugene OR: Wipf & Stock, 2004.

———. *A Second Brithday: A Personal Confrontation with Illness, Pain, and Death*. 1970. Reprinted, The Stringfellow Library. Eugene OR: Wipf & Stock, 2005.

———. *Simplicity of Faith: My Experience in Mourning*. 1982. Reprinted, The Stringfellow Library. Eugene OR: Wipf & Stock, 2005.

Wink, Walter. *Engaging the Powers: Discernment and Resistance in a World of Domination*. The Powers 3. Minneapolis: Fortress, 1992.

Index

Index